THE DAY THE
ROPE BROKE

*The story of a great Victorian tragedy and the end of the
Golden Age of Alpine climbing*

Ronald W Clark

MARA BOOKS
www.marabooks.co.uk

First published by **Martin Secker & Warburg Ltd**. 1965

This edition published in 2008 by **Mara Books**, 22 Crosland Terrace, Helsby, Frodsham, Cheshire WA6 9LY. Tel: 01928 723744

www.marabooks.co.uk
www.northerneyebooks.com

Hardback
ISBN 978 1 902512 12 9
Paperback
ISBN 978 1 902512 17 4

Line drawings by Edward Whymper and the map on page 6 by Anthony Adams-Reilly are taken from: *Scrambles Amongst the Alps in the Years 1860-1869*.

Plates 8 and 9 in the colour section by Irwin Neudorfer

Jacket design and additional photography by Carl Rogers.

Printed by Cromwell Press Ltd, Trowbridge, Wiltshire

CONTENTS

A map of the Matterhorn, Zermatt and Bruil produced by Anthony Adams-Reilly, originally published in: *Scrambles Amongst the Alps in the Years 1860-1869*

Main Characters in order of appearance:

THE REV, JOSEPH M'CORMICK, aged 30

JEAN-ANTONIE CARREL, aged 36, stone mason and guide of Valtournanche, Italy

EDWARD WHYMPER, aged 25, artist and engraver

LORD FRANCES DOUGLAS, aged 18, heir to the Marquess of Queensbury

'OLD PETER' TAUGWALDER, aged 45, guide of Zermatt, Switzerland

THE REV. CHARLES HUDSON, aged 36

MICHEL CROZ, aged 35, guide of Chamonix, Savoy

DOUGLAS HADDOW, aged 19

THE REV. A.G. GIRDLESTONE, aged 33
'YOUNG PETER' TAUGWALDER, aged 21, guide, and son of 'Old Peter'

LIST OF ILLUSTRATIONS

COLOUR PLATES *(between pages 96 & 97)*

AUTHOR'S PREFACE

THE FIRST ASCENT OF THE MATTERHORN IN JULY 1865, and the tragic accident which followed, has remained a subject of compelling interest for a century and a half. It has remained so not only among those who love mountains and think of them often but among a wider public, attracted by a variety of reasons, laudable and perverse. For the conquest of this peak—still formidable in spite of what the French call *la vulgarisation des montagnes*, still supremely beautiful in spite of the superimposed impedimenta of huts and fixed ropes, the nearby railways and sumptuous hotels—involved a rare combination of events and personalities. There was the age old story of man conquering nature and paying a fearful price for success. There was the strange series of coincidences which, as we have appreciated only in recent years, brought three separate parties to Zermatt on the same summer day, intent on the same spectacular ascent. There was the character of Edward Whymper himself, a man who now appears to have been drawn with the inevitability of great tragedy to his own private appointment with destiny on the sloping slabs of the mountain. There was the rivalry of two mountain centres and of two national temperaments simmering just beneath the surface. And there was the continuing theme of dark deeds unrevealed—a theme which seems almost quaintly trivial now that it can, today, be compared with the story of what really happened on the mountain.

It may at first be wondered why such an old tale should be worth re-telling. The truth is that the tale is not old at all. For another factor which has maintained interest in the Matterhorn story is the regularity with which new and significant details have been added to it—from letters, from diaries, from documents and reminiscences only made available throughout the years. Collectively they have brought about something of a sea change.

Edward Whymper gave his own account of the first ascent of the Matterhorn in the immortal *Scrambles*. That book was, however, an artistic masterpiece more than an historical record. Whymper omitted some facts in the unfolding story and he stressed others; he reduced the importance of some players and he magnified his own. At times he has been unduly criticised for this; yet it should be remembered that after 1865 Whymper was treated by much of the world as the greatest mountaineer alive and certainly as the man to whom, almost alone, the conquest of the Matterhorn was due. He had fixed his ambitions on this one ascent with a determination that verged on megalomania; and it was, after all, natural enough that when he began the account of his exploits a few years later, he should already be thinking of himself as the only man who really counted in the story of the great achievement.

Some of his selection, omission and weighting of fact was a matter of deliberate choice, some of it was inevitable. The part played by the Rev. Charles Hudson had been revealed in a lecture given by his friend the Rev. Joseph Mc'Cormick—or 'M'Cormick' as he usually termed himself in the 1860s—but was minimised by Whymper. Girdlestone's part in the long chain of events was also diminished and was high-lighted only in later years, following the generous gift of his letters to the Alpine Club, while the appearance on the scene of Lord Francis Douglas is described in terms which leave many questions unanswered. However, the minutes of the Enquiry into the accident held in Zermatt were released only in 1919—Whymper had not seen them at the time of his death in 1911—and the account of the ascent, and of the accident, given by 'young Peter' Taugwalder during the First World War was published only in 1957. The repercussions of the accident on the British authorities in Berne, and the account of it secured by the British chaplain in Geneva, have been unearthed only for this book.

These are but the more important pieces of evidence that have come to light since Whymper sat down in the quiet of Town House, Haslemere, to write his book. There are many others, most of which have been published only in the mountaineering journals or as obscure, and in some cases privately printed, papers or pamphlets. One difficulty in using this mass of material to reconstruct the events of July 1865, has been its conflicting, and at times directly contradictory, nature. Thus—a small but typical illustration—of those who arrived back in Zermatt after the accident, one reported the time of arrival as 10.30 in the morning, another as 3.00 pm.; other secondary accounts put the time at 2.00 pm. and as 'late on Saturday night'. In most cases the unreliability of memory, the tendency of old men to 'remember with advantages', the unpredictable kinks in the human computer, are sufficient to explain the discrepancies. It has therefore been possible to give, beyond reasonable doubt, an account of what really happened not only on the mountain on July 13th and 14th, but during the preceding days when chance was drawing a trio of separate groups towards Zermatt, and during the tragic aftermath.

The major debt of any author writing a book of this kind is to the specialists who throughout the years have lavished time and scholarship on the unravelling of minute problems. Their works are quoted in the bibliography, but it would be unjust not to mention especially the debt, owed by anyone who writes about the Matterhorn, to the late Captain Farrar and the late Dr. T. Graham Brown; to D. F. O. Dangar and T. S. Blakeney; to Charles Gos; and to Sir Arnold Lunn who has fought the good fight for the Taugwalders with such splendid zest.

Prologue:
Men and the
Matterhorn

NOTHING LIKE IT HAD HAPPENED BEFORE. As the dessert of wild mountain strawberries arrived in the wooden, first floor dining room of Alexander Seiler's Hotel du Mont Rose many of his guests raised their eyes in wonder and disbelief, looked at each other questioningly, made a collective dash for the narrow staircase, descended two steps at a time, napkin in hand, crossed the narrow street outside, and gazed with eyes screened against the light towards the distant chiselled summit of the Matterhorn.

It might be thought that only a natural catastrophe, a *bouleversement* of the proper order of things, could have caused such a movement of men and women soberly dedicated to their mid day muttons. Something very like it had in fact been implied when Seiler, his genial Pickwickian face beaming with good news, had entered the room a moment before.

"Gentlemen! Gentlemen! One can see them! They're close to the Shoulder!" he had announced.

Even to the most sceptical, to those who believed that God would have given men wings had He intended them to visit such summits, the news had meant that the struggle for the Matterhorn was nearing its end.

Now, in the bright sunlight, they were not so sure. Even though it was well past noon, the peaks around the head of the valley still retained a diamond-sharp quality, cut in silhouettes of jet rock and stark snow.

Looking upwards, one was dazzled by the glare. Eyes accustomed to the quieter contrasts of life at low altitudes failed to register. Few could really see anything. Moise Briquet, one of the three Genevese who had entered Zermatt the previous evening, pulled out his short pocket glass. Seiler swore that he would give 500 francs for a telescope.

Only the guides could see. Only the guides could really know what was involved as they described how the small black specks on the uppermost stretch of the ridge above the Hornli were not rocks but men; how they could be seen moving if one watched closely enough; and how this was a day that would have astonished their fathers and shocked their grandfathers, for whom the upper reaches of the Matterhorn had been the abode of spirits, of the Wandering Jew, and of unaccountable things which wise men did not mention.

The men on the Matterhorn were almost at the summit, yet more than one of those watching from the village street must have murmured the old tag about many a slip. Indeed, there now followed an anti-climax. The small figures, the guides averred, could no longer be seen. Seiler threw at least half his attention back to that skilful control of the business which within a single decade had brought him fame not only throughout Switzerland but in that Albion across the seas where men had been gripped with a strange and formidable desire to climb even the most dangerous summits of the Alps.

Twenty minutes passed; then half-an-hour. Only at 1.40pm did there suddenly sprout into view, pin-sharp on the topmost thin crest of the mountain, the figure of a human being. A few seconds later another figure appeared, followed by a third, a fourth, and then three more. For a moment all seven were clearly outlined against the blue sky. Even the oldest and most sceptical of the Zermatt villagers now knew that if there were spirits on the Matterhorn they had at last been joined by men.

There were, of course, two views about both the propriety and the importance of the whole adventure. Not all the guests had come running down the stairs. Nearly half had munched steadily on, convinced that the mountains were beautiful enough from below and that it was most unfitting to hanker for the vantage points of the chamois and the eagle. Even among the inhabitants of Zermatt, there was a difference of opinion, though it would not be unkind to suggest that the division lay mainly in the impact which the new kind of mountain tourist was making upon their lives. For the postmistress, the incident was just one more indication that times were changing. For Seiler it was a great occasion. To one of his staff it was a day which she long remembered. 'All stood about with glasses watching the top.... Then the shouts when they were seen waving the flag ... nothing else was thought of.'

It was a great day for the Valais in general and for Zermatt in particular. Most people were agreed on that as they made their gossiping way upstairs, discussing whether it might not be appropriate to celebrate the success with a small glass of the local liqueur.

And yet. It was difficult to know why but, as the Reverend Joseph M'Cormick was to put it, 'there were no very warm expressions of pleasure at the event'. Perhaps M'Cormick could hardly look on it without a tinge of regret. A muscular Christian whose son Patrick was to become one of the most famous clergymen of the following century, he had arrived at Seiler's only a few hours earlier, hoping to join his friends in just the successful exploit they were now accomplishing.

He had been handed a letter inviting him to 'follow us, if you like'. But his friends had left the previous day. And he had commiserated on his misfortune with young Campbell, the undergraduate he was introducing to the Continent and who now accompanied him indoors. Yet M'Cormick was as likely to praise another's victory as he was to rejoice in his own. He was not the man to fiddle with facts or with feelings, and the lack of those 'very warm expressions of pleasure' at the moment of victory was undoubtedly felt. It was also natural. To the mountaineer, the fact that the Matterhorn had been climbed was like the death of an old enemy, always a sad affair. To the others, determinedly ignorant of why eminent men such as Leslie Stephen, Hereford George, John Ball, should find it necessary to climb mountains at all, the event had a dangerous undercurrent of arrogance; it was almost as if man, now trying to trace his descent back to the humble beasts, had claimed that he would one day be able to move safely under the sea, to fly like birds, or even to find some way of using that energy with which God had created the world in His own good time.

M'Cormick was still discussing plans for the following day with Campbell when young Friedrich Taugwalder came into the hotel with the latest news of the Matterhorn. He was just 15; he had both father and an elder brother on the mountain as guides and he had been scanning it for signs of the descending party.

All he had been able to discern was an avalanche, an avalanche that his brother was to describe, graphically and unrealistically, half a century later, as 'like a small cloud'. But now he was merely brushed aside for his pains.

"An avalanche!" On a warm summer's afternoon, with little fresh snow on the upper slopes—such a thing was impossible! Seiler, good man that he was, had other things to worry about at the height of the season. Moreover, there may still have been, lurking at the back of his mind, a cautious crossed-finger qualification. It was true that the party had set out down the village street at five the previous morning, confident of success, hoping to bivouac high that evening and to reach the summit this following day, July 14th, 1865. Yet the skyline ridge to which one gazed from the meadows above Zermatt was the frontier ridge with Italy. Beyond it lay the slopes up which most of the earlier attempts to climb the Matterhorn had been made. On them, Seiler well knew, brave men had been trying to reach the summit for four days. It was not inconceivable that they too had succeeded, or would succeed before the day was out. Generous as he was, Seiler must still have wondered if the edge of victory was to be blunted.

After all, the issue had hung in the balance for so many years. There had been so many attempts, so much interest among the English. He remembered the day, some while ago, when a reverend gentleman named Wilberforce, the Bishop of Oxford, had been staying at his other hotel, the Mont Cervin. Preaching to the guests in the dining room, Wilberforce had spoken of the Matterhorn as 'a peak as yet untrodden'. And Seiler remembered with some amusement how the guests, knowing that young Mr. Whymper was on the mountain that very day, had waited until the Bishop had left and had then laid a round of bets as to whether he was still right.

However, Seiler had little time for speculation. There were the three Genevese to set on their way with adequate provisions for an ascent of the Dom. The Rev. Joseph M'Cormick and young Mr. Campbell would be leaving at first light but would be back on Sunday evening. The complex tracery of comings and goings, the organisation of food supply, the giving of advice for expeditions projected or merely discussed, the detailed surveillance of a mountain hotel, *touts conforts*, both business proposition and personal family vocation—all this was in mid July at its most complicated and exciting best.

Tomorrow, moreover, the party would be back from the Matterhorn with their story.

Part One
The Cast Assembles

CHAPTER ONE

CARREL THE BERSAGLIERE

O<small>N</small> J<small>ULY</small> 14<small>TH</small>, 1865, <small>THE DAY THAT ENDED THE</small> G<small>OLDEN</small> A<small>GE</small> of mountaineering, the Matterhorn was not the only unclimbed summit of the Alps. In the same group of the Pennines, Mont Collon and the Aiguille de la Za were still virgin. In the range of Mont Blanc, the highest summit of the Grandes Jorasses still awaited an ascent, as did the famous Aiguilles nearby. Farther south in the Dauphiné, there remained Les Bans, a multitude of minor peaks and, more formidable than all others, the huge rock tower of the Meije. Yet all these counted mainly in the material equation; in the more important matter of the mind, none had the reputation of the Matterhorn, or the Cervin as it was also known; none presented so dramatic a challenge, appeared to thrust forward such intractable mountaineering problems or offered to even the most casual wanderer such an object for astonishment, wonder or fear.

The Matterhorn rises to a height of 14,782ft on the main watershed of the Alps, a four-faced rock pyramid isolated from its neighbours on the south-west by the Col du Lion and from those on the south-east by the Théodule Pass, whose high snow ramparts have been crossed since medieval times by adventurous travellers passing from Switzerland to the Val d'Aosta. From the Col du Lion there rises the south-west or Italian ridge of the mountain, a staircase of rocky steps ascending to the horizontal levels of the Italian Shoulder, above which some 800ft of precipices lead to the summit. Beyond, stretching more steeply down, the

Furggen Ridge leads to the Théodule; along both ridges runs the Swiss-Italian frontier and to the south of them lies the deep trough of the Valtournanche, green with Alpine meadows in its upper reaches, thick with chestnut and walnut groves lower down. On the north, the mountain throws down a counterpart of its southern self—the long Swiss ridge leading north-eastwards, dropping, then leading up to the little peak of the Hornli before continuing its descent towards Zermatt in the Vispthal; and a shorter, harsher rock crest which falls from the vertical Zmutt Nose to the crevasses and séracs of the Zmutt Glacier.

On to this simple geometry, the wind and weather which have eroded the mountain have added a complex of lines, angles, sub-ridges, gullies, arêtes and individual features. Two are of prime significance, one to the geography of the peak, the other to the impression which its outline makes on men. For the summit is not a point but a ridge, a snow crest strung for

Whymper's drawing of Jean–Antonie Carrel from Scrambles

a hundred yards between the north-eastern, Swiss summit on which the Swiss and Furggen ridges converge, and the south-western, Italian, summit to which the Italian and Zmutt ridges lead. Their respective heights vary with the season. And to the general pyramidical form the sculpturing of chance has added a final, topmost misalignment, so that the upper thousand feet appear to lean over into space like the frozen crest of a breaking wave.

Most mountains look steeper than they are. Foreshortening increases angles, distance levels the rugosities by which men can climb, and the broken not too difficult slopes appear to the observer as the smoothest of precipices. You can never tell until, as they say, you have rubbed your nose on the rock. To this normal deception of nature the Matterhorn adds the isolation of its bulk, and throughout the passing centuries the mere idea of scaling its slopes retained an air of the ridiculous. Ruskin came to gaze, wonder, write and take the first 'sun picture' of the mountain. In 1855 the scientist Dollfuss-Ausset suggested that by tethering a balloon near its foot and steadily paying out a rope, a man in a basket slung beneath the craft might be raised to the summit. Most men refused to regard the Matterhorn as a mountain that would ever be climbed—even the English who, during the 1850s travelled in ever larger numbers through the Alps and scaled, with the help of the local peasants, one after another of the great peaks. As for the peasants themselves, those who lived quietly in the Vispthal or in the greener depths of the Valtournanche, those wise men shook their heads and turned away. 'There seemed to be a cordon drawn around it, up to which one might go, but no farther', wrote the young Edward Whymper of the situation in 1860. 'Within that invisible line gins and effreets were supposed to exist—the Wandering Jew and the spirits of the damned. The superstitious natives in the surrounding valleys (many of whom firmly believed it to be not only the highest mountain in the Alps, but in the world), spoke of a ruined city on its summit wherein the spirits dwelt; and if you laughed, they gravely shook their heads; told you to look yourself to see the castles and the walls, and warned one against rash approach, lest the infuriate demons from their impregnable heights might hurl down vengeance for one's derision'. Even four years later, when more technically difficult mountains had been climbed, when the last veils of legend were being ripped away from the world above the snowline, one of the finest guides in the Alps could turn to his employer with the entreaty: "Anything but Matterhorn, dear sir."

Jean-Antonie Carrel in later life

Yet by 1860 the first rude attempts had been made to reach the top of the formidable mountain. They had been made by the Italians, from the Valtournanche, by men who were not then professional guides but who were drawn on and upwards by an insatiable curiosity to know what lay on the other side of the hill.

The Valtournanche is today a high road to the most popular ski centre of the Italian Alps. In the mid-19th century it still slumbered in the quiet of an Alpine existence which had altered little since medieval times. Saussure, the man of Mont Blanc, had pushed up the valley at the end of the 18th century and camped on the Théodule for three days, making the first measurements of the Matterhorn's height, studying its geology, tirelessly collecting. Few had followed him, few even of the persistent British, until the Reverend Samuel King penetrated the valley with his indomitable wife and described his experiences in what is now one of the Alpine classics. His successors left the Route Napoléon, marching grandly up the Val d'Aosta towards the little St. Bernard, at the rugged village of Châtillon. They turned uphill through the narrow exit of a steep enclosed valley curving north towards the main watershed of the Alps, a 'blind' valley with poor tracks, few mules or muleteers, little history and humble inns. They rode at places under a trellis work of vines from which the grapes hung in purple clusters. Soon, from the path high above the glacier-cold stream, they caught their first glimpse of a mountain strangely different from the conventional view of the Swiss Matterhorn. Broader, more massive, presenting a great flank of southern precipices, it still appeared the unscaleable mountain *par excellence*. At places the view was contained, as conveniently as a Victorian portrait, within a framework of chestnut and walnut trees, growing in rich profusion on the gentler slopes. Steadily climbing, the traveller would see, after ten miles, the white campanile of Valtournanche itself, a village spread along its single cobble and dung street. Perched finely on a cliff above the river, surrounded by steep slopes of rye, oats and hemp, Valtournanche lay in a setting of distant pines, dotted with chalets and seen against an encirclement of mountain walls, all-enclosing and apparently final.

Here lived Jean-Antoine Carrel, the first man to gaze at the Matterhorn and believe that he could get to the top. Carrel was not, for the greater part of his life, a full-time guide. He was a stone mason by trade, fitted by daily experience with a knowledge of how the living rock reacted to the activities of man, keen of sight, sensitive of touch. It was natural that he should move easily in difficult places, knowing by instinct what pressure was needed between foot and surface to retain contact. It was perhaps natural that he should suspect snow and ice, prefer the bare crags, and make his first efforts to scale the Matterhorn equipped not with the tall ice axe which was by this time coming into general use,

Whymper's illustration of Luc Meynet the 'hunchback' from Scrambles

but with one of the long 'grafios' or metal-tipped ashen sticks with which he and his companions prodded marmots from their holes.

Carrel had been born in 1829 and as a loyal Italian had travelled down through his valley into the great world beyond to fight with the Bersagliere against the Austrians. He had won his sergeant's stripes at Novara at the age of 20, witnessed the rout of the Piedmont troops which caused Charles Albert to die of a broken heart and brought Victor Emmanuel II to the throne. Then he had returned to the solitude of his native valley. He had been swept up in the wave of emotion which was eventually to turn Italy from a rag-bag of medieval states into a coherent nation; and, back in his own village, the same ferment still worked, a not wholly ignoble impulse which made him prefer victory for his own valley rather than for that across the frontier ridge.

Above the village, past the little chapel of Notre Dame de la Garde, the upper reaches of the Valtournanche open out into a broad but upward-sloping green plain. Here lay the chalets of Breuil, standing on the track to the Théodule Pass, over shadowed on the east by the slopes of the Breithorn and on the west by the huge walls of the Matterhorn. Higher still, among the pastures of the Jomein, the Mont Jumont Inn had been opened in 1856 under the control of Signor Favre of Aosta. He had changed the name after a couple of years to the Mont Cervin and here there rested the travellers who crossed the Théodule from Switzerland. They found, as an English traveller noted, 'Good food, good rooms, and great civility. 'What more,' he asked, 'could man desire at 6,600ft above the sea, in the year of grace 1858?'

From the slopes of the Jomein, drawn by the same magnet that has made men sail unknown seas, learn to fly like birds and stretch out to touch the fringe of space itself, Jean-Antoine Carrel looked at the Matterhorn and wondered whether a brave man might not find a way upwards through the torrent of crags.

But others would be needed. One did not attempt things like that alone. Plans were necessary; time free from the quarry when one's companions were also ready; and, above all, the right combination of weather

The Matterhorn rising above Bruil

which would have swept as much snow as possible from the crags and which would offer no threat in the immediate future.

Thus it was only on a summer morning in 1857, as the last stars were growing dim in the sky, that Carrel met two friends at the chalets above Breuil. One of them was his uncle, Jean-Jacques Carrel, a keen-eyed adventurous man who could perhaps see little point in reaching the top of the Matterhorn but who, as a chamois hunter, realised that to know his way among the upper crags might be a useful and even profit earning ability. The other was Aime Gorret, a 'beardless lad of about 20, something between a cleric and a shepherd'.

The trio travelled light-heartedly, almost without plan, with only the vague intention of reaching, at one of its lowest points, the ridge which runs from the Matterhorn, dips towards a series of cols and then rises to the Dent d'Herens, the Italian ridge as it later came to be known. They made their way up one of the small glaciers, and Jean-Jacques quickly got into difficulties, only being saved by the improvised use of a woodman's hatchet and his companions' long 'grafios'.

Soon afterwards they took to the rocks, now on their own ground, and reached the col without difficulty. Here, in some amazement, they looked down the precipitous slopes to the icy wilderness of the Tiefmatten Glacier. They had heard how the pays d'Herens lay behind the Matterhorn, and they expected it to be like their own green valley. Instead, they saw only glaciers hemmed in by rocky heights.

They now sat down to eat; began rolling stones downhill, one of the oldest sports in the world; and then in a leisurely way made their route up the easy ridge to the Tête du Lion. From it, they looked across the Col du Lion, the last dip in the ridge before it begins its long upward sweep towards the summit of the Matterhorn itself. That, no doubt, would be the way. But another day would do. They had found a possible route. And they returned to Breuil contented, Jean-Antoine deciding in his own mind when he would make his next attempt.

But that year, far away in the plains below, the next steps were made towards a united Italy. Men were needed for the complicated movements of march and counter march, for the bloody business of battery and barricade. Jean-Antoine Carrel was recalled to the Army, fought at San Martino and returned a more experienced and able man to the hamlet at the head of the Valtournanche.

As might have been expected, the English had in the meantime been sniffing around the Matterhorn. Elsewhere in the Alps the Swiss, the Germans and the Italians had discovered the mountains as an outlet for their energies long before the English. But from the 1840s onwards the English had come in ever increasing numbers. First there had been the scientists who studied the glaciers and took readings of the way men breathed at high altitudes, much as Saussure had done. Then there came men with no such excuse, clergymen, civil servants, men of letters, lawyers, well-to-do travellers who spent their six or eight weeks travelling at leisure, almost arrogantly sure of themselves. They carried their own conventions with them. There was Edward Shirley Kennedy who sometimes climbed with his man servant Fortunatus following as dutifully close behind as he dared. There was Leslie Stephen who praised one innkeeper because he 'nobly sent a man every day down to Sion for fresh supplies of champagne'. There was C. E. Mathews who once organised a six-course meal followed by coffee and liqueurs in a desolate Alpine hut. Yet to all this they added a cool, directing touch to the native ability of the guides; the majority, judged even by the demanding standards of those who moved in the mountain air for their daily bread, could stand more hardship than most men. What is more, they usually succeeded. During the preceding few years they could, in fact, claim as many 'firsts' as the climbers of all other nationalities put together.

To Carrel it therefore seemed that the English presented the greatest threat to his ambition to be the first man on top of the Matterhorn. From across the Théodule there came reports of how three of them, Alfred, Charles and Sandbach Parker, had even dared to tackle the mountain without guides at all—and had reached about 11,500ft on the Swiss ridge before being forced back.

Here, in Valtournanche, there had arrived two more Englishmen, Vaughan Hawkins and a resolute scientist, Professor Tyndall, a man of iron who appeared to have Carrel's determination to be first to the top. Jean-Jacques, incredibly it must have seemed to his nephew, had actually gone with their local Swiss guide and helped them to find a way up the Italian ridge until, at about 13,000ft, they had been stopped by the difficulties of the rocks.

Jean-Antoine himself roamed at will over the lower slopes of the mountain, fitting in his expeditions between work as a quarryman, getting to know the individual features of the mountain; occasionally going quite high up the Italian ridge but never finding time, or the right weather, or the necessary companion, or the needed combination of circumstances, to press up higher than the wretched Englishmen. He must do so one day and he must do it soon.

Then, in the August of 1861, Carrel found himself faced, in the village of Valtournanche, with a tall blunt young Englishman who brusquely demanded whether he would go with him on the Matterhorn. There was something about this Englishman's manner that was compelling, something that warned Carrel of an adversary more dangerous than the others, even though his only companion was a man from down the valley whom Carrel held in little regard. Yes, of course he would go. But he would want 20 francs a day, win or lose, an absurd price that any reasonable man would reject.

The Englishman assented.

Well, demanded Carrel, he would of course also have to take his companion—and he summoned forth an unknown friend who was fortuitously present in the building. Now at last the Englishman declined, and continued on his way up to Breuil.

Carrel enquired at the inn along the street. The name, he was told, was Whymper—Edward Whymper. He was young, he was inexperienced. He was unlikely to do much. Carrel doubted that, correctly sensing some ruthless concentration in the young man's gaze and gait that made him different from the rest. With little delay he sought out his uncle and persuaded him that action must be taken. Shortly afterwards both men marched out from Valtournanche up the road to Breuil.

There at the inn Carrel learned that his fears had been justified. Edward Whymper had tried to engage a second man, but had been unsuccessful. Only old Peter Taugwalder from Zermatt had offered to go—and his terms had been even more outrageous than Carrel's. "Two hundred francs, succeed or not."

Yet in spite of it all—it is difficult not to imagine the mixture of contempt and annoyance on Carrel's face—in spite of it all, the Englishman had been determined to go on. He wanted to get as near to the Matterhorn as possible before nightfall and would even now be sleeping rough with his solitary guide, somewhere up in one of the higher chalets.

Carrel and his uncle knew how to deal with that. They, too, could sleep rough. They made their way up the path and to avoid recriminations attempted to bypass a glowing campfire outside one of the upper chalets. They were unsuccessful, and almost a decade later Whymper remembered and recorded the details of their encounter.

"Oh, oh, you have repented," he called out as he saw their shadowy figures.

"Not at all, you deceive yourself," Carrel replied. "Why, then, have you come up here?"

"Because we ourselves are going on the mountain tomorrow."

"Then it is not necessary to have more than three?" came Whymper's reply.

"Not for us," Carrel shouted back as they moved on and upwards into the darkness.

They bivouacked higher up the mountain and moved on at first light, the Englishman safely below them. They got on to the main ridge and reached the 'Chimney', a steep slab of rock between equally smooth containing walls, which Carrel rightly expected would halt even the best of men. They succeeded in passing the spot which Jean-Jacques pointed out as the highest reached by Hawkins and Tyndall the previous year. They climbed at least 300ft higher, as far as time and caution allowed, and here Carrel cut out on the rock with the iron spike of his axe the date, a cross, his initials, and the rough design of a tiara. Here, on rock untouched by man since the world began, Carrel put his mark of ownership. Below him, Whymper was brought to a halt at the Chimney.

This summer of 1861 marked the opening of a determined campaign against the Matterhorn. The Englishmen came back—the next year and the next, Whymper and Tyndall each succeeding in getting a little higher, each using Carrel and each realising how the Italian resented the intrusion of others into what he considered his own private world.

Then, in 1863, the situation was miraculously altered. For to Carrel in Valtournanche there came not an Englishman but an Italian, Guiseppe Torelli. He came as emissary from a group which had met in Turin earlier in the year with the aim of forming an Italian Alpine Club. They wished, Torelli explained, to inaugurate the Club by carrying out some great expedition which would make the Italian sun shine more brightly in the Alpine firmament. What better than an ascent of the Matterhorn? And who better to organise this for them than Jean-Antoine Carrel?

For Carrel, indeed, nothing could be better. The Matterhorn, he felt, was a gift within his bounty. And how fitting that he should present it to Italy.

Torelli spoke with Carrel for an hour, and it was arranged that the guide should visit Biella, down in the foothills, and there discuss the matter in more detail with Quintino Sella, the statesman of whom it was later to be written that he did two things 'gave Rome to Italy and founded the Italian Alpine Club.'

No record remains of that interview, but one can imagine Carrel standing hat in hand in the flagged hallway of Sella's fine house on the San Gerolamo estate outside Biella, and then working out with him the problems of such an expedition, the stores that would be required, the cost, the number of guides, the need to concert everything so that the quickest advantage could be taken of the weather. All this, and much more, had to be settled, for it was realised that a major effort, buttressed by organisation of an almost military size and efficiency, would be necessary.

Felice Giordano would be the best man to make the attempt, Sella suggested, and the following spring he would meet Carrel in Valtournanche and make final arrangements. So far, so good. Giordano came. Providence, in the shape of the weather, now intervened. In 1864 no attempts were made to climb the Matterhorn—even by the English.

Thus events hung fire until 1865. Early that summer Carrel began to reconnoitre the mountain once more. It had been suggested that stanchions, fixed ropes, many ingenious devices, even explosives to blast a way, might be used when Giordano came up from the plains for the great ascent. Only Carrel could really give an expert opinion. It was necessary to make many journeys on the lower slopes of the mountain, and on July 7th, 1865, Carrel, Jean-Joseph Maquignaz and two others were returning from one of them. They had been unable to go high. The mists had descended, they had been forced down to the meadows of Breuil, and they now made their way back along the track to Valtournanche.

Giordano, Carrel realised, would soon be sending further instructions, maybe in a week or so, maybe in days. They surely would not fail this time, after all their plans, all their preparations, all the knowledge of the mountain he had so hardily gathered during the last eight years? Surely before many weeks had passed the glorious struggle would be over?

Carrel's thoughts were not unique. As he and his companions strode down the Valtournanche on that summer morning, at least four other men believed that the hour of the Matterhorn was approaching. Two were at that very moment on the slopes of Mont Blanc, 40 miles to the west; one was traversing a high peak into the Vispthal only a few miles away across the frontier; the fourth was already descending into the Valtournanche from one of the ridges enclosing the upper valley. Chance, operating in a way which only blind history would have dared to contrive, was to bring all four together. All four were to succeed. One was to survive.

CHAPTER TWO

THE HEIR TO
THE MARQUESS OF
QUEENSBURY

THE HAMLET OF ZINAL LIES SOME 13 MILES NORTH OF BREUIL, across the frontier, across the main watershed of the Alps, at the head of the beautiful Val d'Anniviers which runs up from the Rhone Valley near Sierre. In the summer of 1865 only a rough mule track led through the lower gorges to Vissoie, the principal village in the valley, past Mission and Ayer, the last permanently occupied hamlets, and then through rising pine forests to the clusters of houses which formed Zinal. From the pastures above the buildings one could see that the head of the valley was ringed with some of the most dramatic peaks of the Pennine Alps—the Grand Cornier and the Dent Blanche to the south, the Obergabelhorn, the Rothorn, and the pyramid of the Weisshorn curving round to the east in a ridge of splendid summits.

Here there arrived on July 6th Lord Francis William Bouverie Douglas, younger brother of the Marquess of Queensberry, aged only 18 yet assured and masterful, standing on the verge of what promised to be a brilliant career. The 8th Marquess, about to celebrate his majority this month, had succeeded to the title on the death of their father seven years before and while John Sholto Douglas was thus destined for management of the family estates, his brother had chosen the Army. It had been a good choice. Only a few weeks ago he had passed out at the top of the Army examination list, some 500 marks ahead of the nearest among his 118 competitors. Now, for just four weeks, he could relax, returning to the upper Val d'Anniviers from which he had made his first Alpine ascent two years previously. This year he was more ambitious. He had limbered up in the Oberland and now came to Zinal with the aim of making the first ascent of the Ober Gabelhorn. Then, before setting out for home on the 19th, he would cut a dash for the Matterhorn, that mountain which had so exercised his seniors.

Through the whole history of mountaineering there has passed a constant succession of such exceptional, gifted young men, carrying their own haloes of good luck and success, moving easily within an enveloping cloak of charm, confidently able to mix with all who came their way,

Lord Frances Douglas

The Ober Gabelhorn from above Zermatt

as comfortable with the scientists and the gaitered bishops they have met in Alpine inns as with the guides in whom their *élan* has awakened some fellow feeling bridging differences of class, country and culture. They have had, perhaps, no very deep feeling for the mountains. They have not climbed to satisfy their souls; they have invoked no humbug; they have known that while it is good to be first it is not everything; they have looked on mountaineering as a game and have, without inhibitions, 'loved the game beyond the prize'. Thus, Lord Francis Douglas no doubt looked at the Matterhorn.

He was of medium height, toughly built but nimble, with a shock of dark hair brushed well back, and upward slanting eyebrows that gave him a slightly demonic look. He was a good goer, in trim condition, and only slightly handicapped by a painful sore on the side of one heel which had caused him to remove a circle of leather from the side of his shoe. All might be possible for such a man.

With Douglas at Zinal there were two guides. One was Joseph Vianin, a man from Ayer a few miles down the valley. The other was Peter Taugwalder, 'old Peter' as he was known to distinguish him from his son, 'young Peter'. Bushy-browed, with the slow, sure and slightly ambling gait of the man born to walking uphill, Taugwalder was aged 45, a Zermatt man who during the previous few years had worked with many of the finest amateurs of the day. Their opinions on him varied, and great controversy has raged over the exact position which he should occupy on the ladder of ability which posterity has erected for the guides of the Golden Age. Yet of one thing there can be no doubt. Of all the Zermatt guides, only Taugwalder believed by this date that the Matterhorn might be climbed. He appears to have had no particularly romantic feelings about it. If he climbed for his country or his valley, he climbed also as a business. He thought that the Swiss side might 'go', and thus provide one more expedition for the tourists. It was a worthy enough desire for any man dutifully employed at his trade, art or craft, and he had no doubt been suitably satisfied when Douglas, walking into Zermatt ten days earlier, had mentioned an ascent of the Matterhorn as an enterprise with which he wished to round off this particular visit to the Alps.

It is here that the first 'if only' creeps into the story. If only Douglas had decided that he was ready, there and then, for the Matterhorn. If only the weather had not continued to wreathe it in clouds while the lesser peaks surrounding the upper Vispthal remained clear. If only old Peter had urged him that no time was to be wasted, that he should camp out at the foot of the mountain if need be, in order to seize the first chance that came.

Yet no such sudden dramatic effort was made. Before Douglas was to come to grips with the Matterhorn there was to be a time consuming prologue during which he was to spend a week and a half on the nearby peaks. Had any incident of those eleven days been omitted, the story would have been different.

As it was, while the Matterhorn waited, Douglas and his guides set out to tackle various summits which rise from the ridge separating the upper Vispthal from the Val d'Anniviers. On the 6th, Douglas decided that they should make a third attempt on the Ober Gabelhorn, a peak on which success had so far eluded them. But it should be made from the Zinal side, and they had therefore to cross the ridge between the two valleys. On the pass they had a surprise. For as Taugwalder was examining the mountain and was saying that 'we should get up easily from this side', they heard sounds above them and beheld on the top of the Ober Gabelhorn a flag and three men.

Douglas's note in the hotel book at Zinal shows he had no idea that the party consisted of Horace Walker, A. W. Moore and their guide Jakob Anderegg. But he did know that here was one 'first' which had escaped him, and he might well have turned back to Zermatt there and then. Walker and Moore arrived in the village that night, and had Douglas done the same there is little doubt that back in the valley they would have exchanged experiences, discussed possibilities. They might even have decided to try their communal luck on the Matterhorn.

As it was, Douglas and the guides continued down to Zinal. Here they reprovisioned, and agreed to leave for the Ober Gabelhorn at 2.30am on the following morning, July 7th. In the dark they retraced their steps for a part of the route, then bore up towards their peak; after six hours heavy going they found themselves at the foot of the rocks leading to the summit. Four hours more were needed, over difficult ground, up steep ice slopes, before they were at last on the highest point. Yet here, unaccountably to them, they could see no footprints of the previous party. Without further thought Douglas and Taugwalder, still roped, 'sat down to dine' on the very summit itself in Douglas's words.

'All of a sudden I felt myself go,' he recorded the following day, 'and the whole top fell with a crash thousands of feet below, and I with it as far as the rope allowed.'

For the summit was but a huge cornice, curling over into space, its dangers more easily perceived by the party which had approached it from the other side.

Taugwalder fell too, slipping past Douglas until he also was brought

The two Taugwalders: Young Peter (left) and Old Peter (right)

up harshly by the rope. Vianin, the other guide, had casually walked a few feet away a second or so earlier. He was still roped to the other two and as they dropped away with a shout of surprise, he turned and braced himself against the shock. The rope held. So did Vianin, possibly aided by the friction of the rope as it cut deeply into the snow. Yet he must, Douglas estimated, have held a total weight of 23 stone, and was able to hold it while the two men scrambled back to the broken cornice.

It had been a shaking experience. Nevertheless, in spite of Douglas's charitable statement that Taugwalder had 'showed himself a first-rate guide', it suggested a casualness in old Peter's attitude. More experienced men might have felt it unwise, after this, to leave to him important matters of leadership, the choice of route, or the choice of ropes.

However, all was well. At 1.30pm they set off down the rocks to Zermatt, on a journey that did not end until nine hours later as they marched into the village under the light of a full moon. They had been out for 20 hours and they could now rest while Douglas decided what he really wanted to do next—whether, in fact, the time was ready for his attempt on the Matterhorn. The following day was Saturday, July 8th and one can surmise that he spent it in the indeterminate manner of a man forced into inactivity by natural tiredness yet anxious to be out on the mountains; half enjoying the leisure, half regretting it, taking his ease yet realising that this was not really the way to be spending the time.

Zermatt was a pleasant place for an off-day, still linked with the outside world only by a rough track, although this was even now being worked up into a road. Well within memory the only place where a traveller could rest had been Dr. Lauber's humble house, transformed into an inn in 1839 and enlarged nine years later into a structure which contained half a dozen or so bedrooms above a large eating room with rough deal tables and benches. The food, it was said, consisted of 'soup made of mutton, then mutton boiled, mutton roasted, and then mutton broiled'. Such primitive conditions were soon changed, first by the opening of the Hotel du Mont Cervin in 1852; then, more decisively, by Lauber's sale of his little inn two years later to Alexander Seiler. In one respect Seiler was lucky, since he took over the establishment, renaming it the Hotel du Monte Rosa, just as the British wave of Alpine enthusiasm broke over the Valais. Under his inspired management it became 'the club room of Zermatt'; from it there set out almost all the parties which in the following decade first climbed the peaks surrounding the head of the valley. Its proprietor was both host and friend, advising and arranging for extra guides where necessary, ensuring that provisions were ready on time, holding blankets and similar stores available, a man much more than hotelier who had become, by 1865, an Alpine father confessor to a clientele which was largely British. 'Other landlords rose and vanished, bankrupt or glad to escape bankruptcy', it was later written. 'Seiler flourished. He was never spoiled.'

It was in such an atmosphere that Douglas spent the weekend. Nothing is known of his exact movements between his return to Zermatt on the Friday night and his departure from the village the following Tuesday morning. But he had until the end of the week to accomplish what he wanted. He had set his heart on the Matterhorn. And it is reasonable to suppose that he spent a long weekend taking advice, watching the weather which still obscured the mountain with clouds, reluctant to embark on any expedition which might break into his plans for this one major enterprise with which he hoped to end the season.

It seems certain that he sent Taugwalder out to reconnoitre the mountain once again. And it seems certain that someone at Zermatt spoke to him of the Italian side from which most previous attempts had been made. They will also have mentioned, perhaps with a touch of awe, the name of Jean-Antoine Carrel. And to a determined practical man such as Douglas, imbued with the military maxim of always attacking with the strongest available forces, one possibility will obviously have loomed up. Why not reinforce Taugwalder with Carrel? Two heads would be better than one. There might, of course, be problems, there might be friction, but all that would have to be dealt with later on. The first thing, surely, was to get Carrel's services.

All this is surmise. But we do know that early on the morning of Tuesday, July 11th, Douglas set out from Zermatt. With him went Joseph Taugwalder, the second of 'old Peter's' three sons. Both men were travelling light and they made good time up the track which goes over steadily rising ground towards the Théodule Pass. Beyond it lay Breuil and, Douglas hoped, a Jean-Antoine Carrel who would help take him to the top of the mountain whose east face he could see across the white stretches of the Furggen Glacier.

Yet even as Douglas breasted with his companion the slopes leading towards the Théodule there was coming up from Visp another party whose ambitions were also fixed on the Matterhorn.

It was led by the Rev. Charles Hudson who, a few days earlier, as the actors in the Matterhorn drama were being jostled into their starting positions, was high on the slopes of Mont Blanc.

CHAPTER THREE

THE CLERGYMAN FROM THE CRIMEA

FROM THE CLUSTER OF HOUSES OF PRAZ CONDUITS, a little below Chamonix, there mounted in 1865 a good mule path which traversed a pine forest and then broke out on to open pastures, rising all the time until it eventually reached the Pierre Pointue. Here, by a gigantic stone which had been a landmark for early travellers, there had been constructed a modest inn, some 6,720ft up and a useful jumping-off point for those making the ascent of Mont Blanc by the usual route. And here, on the evening of July 6th there assembled a happy, almost family, party of six English, two guides, and one dog.

The leadership rested firmly on the shoulders of the Rev. Charles Hudson, aged 36, possibly the finest amateur mountaineer of his time, the man who only the previous day had made the second ascent of the neighbouring Aiguille Verte with another member of the party, Thomas Stuart Kennedy. Aged 24, already an experienced mountaineer, Kennedy was accompanied by his dog and by his young wife for this was a honeymoon visit to the Alps. The fourth English member of the party was the Rev. Joseph M'Cormick, an old friend of Hudson, a double Blue standing more than six foot in his socks. Completing the British contingent were Douglas Hadow, just 18, and young Campbell, former pupils of Hudson and M'Cormick respectively who were being initiated into the mysteries of the High Alps. As guides there were Michel Croz whose employer, John Birkbeck, now lay ill in Chamonix, and Peter Perren.

Hudson dominated the party at the Pierre Pointre as he dominated, by sheer force of character, most of those with whom he mixed. Looking at portraits of him, it is possible to see what the muscular Christians of the 19th century were really like—questioning and cool, humble and confident. The face which the photographers have fixed for all time is that of the man who could genuinely pray upon the mountains for success without appearing impertinent. He thought. He suffered. And so he was, as incorruptible by victory as by defeat.

Hudson was tall and well built, wearing his hair long and with thick sideboards after the fashion of the period. Full, voluptuous lips and fine deep-set eyes contributed to the delicate, almost feminine, impression given by his face, an impression belied by the activities for which he had become famous. A north countryman, Hudson had from youth demonstrated those powers of hard going which the north sometimes produces to an astonishing degree. At the age of 17 he had averaged 27 miles a day throughout a walking holiday in Cumberland, a county where miles are apt to come unaccountably long. At St. John's, which he entered in 1847, he brought the college boat to the head of the river, won 'the fours', pulled stroke to the winning 'pairs' and divided the 'sculls' with a Trinity man, the race being pronounced a dead heat. As stroke, it was recalled, he pulled so much stronger than his companions that an iron rudder was fixed to the boat, yet the race was still the fastest on record. This physical heartiness was but a tool to be used. 'He considered', remarked a friend, 'that the cultivation of athletic powers gave him a sympathy with young men, and an influence over them, which he could not otherwise attain; and he was sincerely desirous to make his bodily powers subservient to this end.' He possessed no startling intellect. He had great good intentions, and it was perhaps inevitable that he should drift into Holy Orders; as inevitable that on the outbreak of the Crimean War he should leave his curacy at St. Mary's, Bridgnorth, enrol as a Chaplain with the Army, and spend the winter of 1854 in the Crimea, living hard and, after the fall of Sebastopol, making an adventurous trip across Armenia with the intention of climbing Ararat.

Hudson returned to England, and throughout the following decade established himself as a leader in the new sport of Alpinism during its Golden Age. Like Lawrence of Arabia half a century later, he developed the practice of 'hardening himself by constant neglect'. Asked why he left for a high pass at three in the afternoon in the middle of winter, he replied that 'it was in order to be compelled to spend the night in the snow.' On one occasion he walked 86 miles in 24 hours, and after a brief rest set out on another excursion. His topographical instinct, which gave him 'an intuitive general notion of the lay of the country', enabled him

The Rev. Charles Hudson

to make a new route up Mont Blanc—the first to be carried out without the aid of guides. He made the first ascent of the highest summit of Monte Rosa and brought his wife to Zermatt on their honeymoon in 1862. More than once his mind turned speculatively towards the Matterhorn, God's great pinnacle which had so far repulsed all comers.

In the spring of 1865, the Vicar of the village of Skillington, Lincolnshire, as Hudson had by that time become, invited two men to his home to discuss plans for the summer. The first of them was T. S. Kennedy, a rare, distinguished all-rounder who succeeded in most things he tackled almost as of aristocratic right. He was a fine sportsman and skilful draughtsman, keen rider to hounds and good musician.

Kennedy first saw the Matterhorn in the summer of 1858, at the age of 17, and both then and two years later cogitated on how it might be climbed. Unlike most of the others, he ruled out the Italian side and from the first thought that the Swiss ridge offered the better chance. He could see, however, that high up on the mountain, where the final slopes steepened, there were difficult rock stretches; and he believed, in his innocence, that they might be less difficult in winter—since a rock pitch can sometimes be made easier by masking snow. He arrived at Zermatt in January 1862, found the village shuttered for the winter and, not without some trouble, obtained lodgings with the curé. Then, with old Peter Taugwalder and Peter Perren he had taken supplies up to the Schwarzsee Chapel beneath the Hornli, spent a bleak night there, and set out the following morning to face a mountain plastered with snow and ice, beset by high winds, and wearing a costume of complete impregnability.

To combat the weather, Kennedy wore great-coat and belt over his usual clothes, fur cap and woollen scarf over his head. The guides were equally muffled against weather in which one did not usually go farther from home than was necessary. Astonishingly, they reached nearly 11,000ft, scrambling without undue difficulty up the steepening Swiss ridge until the weather combined with the snow conditions to halt them. 'Still no one seemed to like to be the first to give in,' Kennedy later wrote, 'till a gust fiercer than usual forced us to shelter for a time behind a rock.

Immediately it was tacitly understood that our expedition must now end; but we determined to leave some memento of our visit, and after descending a considerable distance we found a suitable place with loose stones of which to build a cairn. In half an hour a tower six feet high was erected; a bottle with the date was placed inside, and we retreated as rapidly as possible.'

Kennedy did not renew his attempt on the Matterhorn. Then, at Easter 1865, he visited Hudson and the two men planned their campaign for the coming season. Kennedy, it was true, would be on his honeymoon but his wife could thus be introduced to the delights of the Alps and would understand better when, during the years to come, her husband felt obliged to disappear for an annual bout of mountaineering. First the party would go to Chamonix where the Aiguille Verte, a massive rock spire on the flanks of Mont Blanc, still remained unclimbed, even by that man Whymper who for the last few years had been claiming Alpine victories, one after another, with the confident assurance of a good shot knocking down birds without wasting a barrel. Then they would turn to the Matterhorn.

No record exists of what passed between Hudson and Kennedy as they planned the ascent of the most important unclimbed peak of the Central Alps. But it seems likely that Kennedy's experience on the mountain three years previously combined with Hudson's eye for country to destroy the picture which had so far protected the Swiss side of the mountain from most attempts. That Swiss ridge was not nearly so formidable as men had imagined, Kennedy must have averred. Hudson, thinking back now to how the slopes had looked when they descended Monte Rosa a few years earlier, tended to agree. If the Swiss ridge dropped so many thousand feet in so many hundred yards, it should not be too steep at any one place; if the east face riding out from it held snow as well as it certainly did, then it could not be so precipitous. It had all been an illusion. Let everyone else concentrate on the southern slopes, on the Italian ridge. They would try the Swiss side. And if there were, in fact, any short dangerous places, then it might be possible to pass them with the aid of something which Hudson himself had devised—a metal cable whose uses would be even more ingenious than those of the grappling hooks and similar contraptions which Mr. Whymper was beginning to use on the mountains.

Thus it was arranged, and Hudson was able to maintain confidently to his next visitor 'that the Matterhorn could be conquered, and that from the Zermatt side'. This next visitor was the Rev. Joseph M'Cormick, aged 29, a former friend from Cambridge, an assistant minister at St. Stephen's, Marylebone, who already had one claim to fame—that he had 'hit a fast bowler to leg on Parker's Piece and run nine for it'. His experience of mountaineering was slight, but his enthusiasm was as great as his athletic powers, and he was freely invited to join Hudson and his friends. It was not quite clear how many of them there would be, but it seemed that young Birkbeck was coming, young Birkbeck whom Hudson had introduced to the Alps four years previously and who had miraculously escaped an 1,800ft fall from the Col de Miage. M'Cormick might bring one or more pupils, while Hudson remembered a Douglas Hadow who had visited the Alps for the first time the previous year, was a tremendous goer, and who might agree to join in.

It is likely that they totted up the 'possibles' for the Matterhorn. Hudson and Kennedy of course; M'Cormick and Birkbeck if all went well. Then there was George Joad who, ten years before, at the age of only 16, had gone to the Aiguille du Garter with Hudson, then his tutor; who had made the first ascent of Mont Blanc by the Bosses with him in 1859; and who would be coming out to the Alps that summer—but they could settle all the details at a later date. There would, it could clearly be seen, be no lack of candidates for the Matterhorn in the summer of 1865.

M'Cormick left Hudson having agreed that they should meet at the end of June, somewhere in the Alps. As it turned out, they met in London, on June 26th. For during the interval M'Cormick had applied to the Colonial and Continental Church Society for a few weeks' chaplaincy in Switzerland, and had been given Grindelwald for the first two Sundays in July, Zermatt for the other three.

In London, Hudson introduced Douglas Hadow, a tall energetic youth of 19, who had just left Harrow and had been intrigued by his sight of the Alps the previous year; now he was out to do great things. M'Cormick brought his pupil Campbell, and the four men travelled together to Paris. Here the party split, Hudson and Hadow taking the train to Geneva, enroute for Chamonix. M'Cormick and Campbell made for Grindelwald and arranged to join the others in a few days' time at Argentière, the little village at the head of the Chamonix Valley.

M'Cormick arrived in Grindelwald in time to officiate on Sunday, July 2nd, and to see how plans for the English church were progressing now that Herr Bohren of 'The Adler' had given a suitable site near the hotel. Fifteen minutes after midnight, he set out on foot with Campbell for the 13-mile walk to Interlaaken. Here they took the steamer to Thun, then the train to Berne, changed there for Lausanne and eventually arrived in Martigny at 9.30pm that night. The following morning they crossed the 7,231ft Col de Balme from the Valais into Savoy and marched down into Argentière—only to find a note from Hudson saying that his party had gone to Chamonix.

Here, once again, they found that Hudson had moved on. They found, also, that they had all lost the Aiguille Verte to Whymper who had got there before them and climbed the mountain on the day that Kennedy and Hudson met in Chamonix. Now Whymper had moved on, as usual a figure just a few steps ahead of the older and more experienced players in the game. M'Cormick, even with the greatest charity, may have thought it somewhat unjust.

This, however, was not the only thing to worry about. Young Birkbeck had arrived, but was ill and about to return to England, a disappointing development even though he had kindly agreed that Michel Croz, the guide he had hired for July, should transfer his services to the Hudson party.

This, in itself, was but the first strange turn of the wheel. For only an unlikely misunderstanding had made it possible in the first place for Birkbeck to hire this daring exponent of new ascents, difficult passes, tremendous expeditions. Michel Croz came from the nearby hamlet of Le Tour where he had been born 35 years previously. For many years he had rubbed along first as porter, then as guide, making little mark. Then his career blazed up. He climbed with the leading mountaineers of the day—William Mathews, who described him as 'only happy when upwards of 10,000ft high', Francis Fox Tuckett, T. G. Bonney, Adams-Reilly and A. W. Moore. He made the first ascent of Monte Viso, that mountain whose summit hangs like a white lantern above the north Italian plain. In one roistering campaign with Whymper and Moore in the Dauphiné he made the first ascent of the Ecrins and the first crossings of the Brèche de la Meije and the Col de la Pilatte. For above all he climbed with Whymper, the impetuous man after his own heart to whom he was above the range of ordinary mortals. And at the end of the triumphant campaign in 1864 Whymper had engaged Michel Croz for the whole of the next summer.

Then there had come an oversight that was to play its special part in the events of 1865. For Whymper had forgotten to confirm the engagement until April. Croz had sent him no reminder, and had therefore felt himself free to take all offers that came. One arrived from Birkbeck, who engaged him from June 27th, leaving his services free for Whymper only until that date. Birkbeck had not in fact arrived by the 27th and Whymper, setting out for the Aiguille Verte, would dearly have liked Croz to go with him. But the guide held to his word. He would await his new employer, who arrived only to succumb to illness, to regret that he must return to England, and to leave Michel Croz kicking his heels while Whymper continued over the tops and far away. It also left him free for transfer to Hudson's party.

By the time that M'Cormick arrived, Croz had therefore led Hudson on the successful second ascent of the Verte. And at breakfast in the Hotel de l'Union at Chamonix on the morning of July 6th, M'Cormick heard from his friends how the attempt had been a glorious success. It had been a large party—of some significance in the light of what was to follow on the Matterhorn—consisting of Hudson and Kennedy, the Rev.

George Hodgkinson, a 49 year-old schoolmaster friend of Birkbeck who appears to have joined the party quite fortuitously; Michel Croz; two other guides; and Kennedy's small dog who successfully made the ascent and slept on the summit while everyone else admired the view.

It had been a magnificent expedition, a splendid start to the season, and one can imagine Hudson explaining how they had overcome great difficulties before reaching the summit where Croz, trembling with excitement, had turned to them with the words, 'Voila, messieurs, l'Aiguille Verte entièrement et complètement' as a gun on the Flégère had boomed out the news of their triumph to the valley of Chamonix.

'The day was perfect' Kennedy later wrote, 'a lighted candle might have been held in the air.' They had spent more than an hour basking on the summit and had turned to the descent only in the early afternoon. Hudson had come down last on the rope, acting as sheet-anchor, an unusual role for an amateur and one later explained by Kennedy. 'His object

Douglas Hadow

was, undoubtedly, to render himself as independent and self-reliant as possible, and in this he had succeeded to an extent greater than I have ever seen in any other Englishman. He was almost as great as a guide.' It was getting dark by the time the party reached their bivouac at the rocks of the Couvercle, but after an hour's rest they set off down the glacier by the light of the moon. Soon after two in the morning they were hammering on the doors of the Montanvert, where Kennedy and one of the guides decided to stay until morning. But after a bottle of champagne had been savoured by all, Hudson and Hodgkinson continued down the path to Chamonix into which they strode soon after 5am.

And now, Hudson explained to M'Cormick, he was going to take a nap. Then all would be ready for them to start off once again in the afternoon—up to the Pierre Pointue and then onwards the following day for a brisk ascent of Mont Blanc.

By the summer of 1865 much of the lustre which had previously covered an ascent of Mont Blanc had been brushed off by the scores of travellers who had reached the summit. Yet the mountain still rose some 12,366ft above Chamonix. It was still guarded by great bastions of snow whose extent could in certain conditions blanket the efforts of even the most vigorous mountaineers, bring them to a halt and, if luck went the wrong way, expose them to the killing conditions which exist at only arm's length on all high mountains. Climbing Mont Blanc was still an adventure, and in the afternoon of July 6th Hudson came up to M'Cormick's room so that they might pray together for success.

He was, his friend later wrote, the sort of man who 'felt that the day which was not begun with a fair amount of time expended in prayer, a study of the Bible and meditation, was not spent satisfactorily'. Now he was to brace himself spiritually for the coming ascent, to be made with his young and untried companion Hadow, as well as with the experienced Kennedy and the eager M'Cormick.

"Our strength of body is from Thee" he began. "Be with us as we make use of it. Prosper us in our new excursion. If it would do us harm to go up this mountain if—we would be puffed up with pride; if our bodies or souls would get any injury—frustrate our expedition. We desire to be as little children in Thy hands, going or staying, as it pleaseth Thee."

Now, he felt, they were properly prepared. The two men went downstairs and explained to a slightly disbelieving proprietor that they hoped to be back by the following evening. At four o'clock in the afternoon they set out for the Pierre Pointue.

With Hudson and M'Cormick there were Hadow, Campbell and Kennedy, Mrs. Kennedy, Croz and Peter Perren, and within three hours they had mounted 3,300ft and reached what was then the small inn standing on the rocks below the Glacier des Bossons. The party was both large and unexpected, and that evening some of its members slept on mattresses laid on the dining room floor. They had only a short night, for at 1.00am they rose, and all except Mrs. Kennedy and Campbell set off, their host taking them up to the edge of the ice with his glacier lantern.

Hudson's ascent of Mont Blanc with young Hadow and the rest of the party during the hours that followed had a somewhat rollicking, schoolboyish air. It was a feat of athleticism as much as anything else. And it was to provide Hadow with the credentials which were to be his passport to triumph and disaster.

They made their way up the Glacier des Bossons by the light of the stars which soon began to fade into the splendour of an Alpine dawn. All was visible before they reached the rocks of the Grands Mulets and the small hut whose fleas, as John Ball once put it, 'make up for long fasting by unusual activity'. Here there were signs of recent occupation and it was generally agreed that another climber must have left for the summit an hour or so previously.

'The true British instinct came upon us that he must be caught before reaching the top', Kennedy wrote, and after a brief halt for a first breakfast they turned upwards through the snow towards the huge white névé of the Grand Plateau. They were soon pushing themselves; someone—probably M'Cormick—showed signs of feeling the pace, and it was decided to separate into two parties. Peter Perren led the first rope with Hadow behind him and Kennedy bringing up the rear. Hudson followed with M'Cormick and Croz.

It was now quite clearly a race, and they were soon across the Grand Plateau and at the foot of the Corridor, the rising snow-filled trough leading towards the summit. Perren's party had by this time gained half an hour on Hudson and the others, pressing on, in Kennedy's words, 'with that sweet sense of innate power and endurance which is only attained at the expense of much severe labour'.

They tackled the great slope with all speed and were quickly high enough to meet a great mass of white clouds boiling up from Italy. Soon, for the first time, they saw the figures ahead of them, and increased their speed.

At last they reached the point where they could safely cast off the rope. Here Kennedy turned to Hadow and asked how he felt, reminding him that they were now some 14,000ft up, a height at which most travellers began to succumb to the altitude. 'He only laughed,' commented Kennedy, 'adding that this was the first glacier mountain he had ever ascended, excepting the Buet; his strength and endurance were extraordinary.'

They plodded on and up, higher and higher, still hoping that they could wipe out the distance between themselves and the figures ahead. They almost succeeded. But on the last few hundred feet they saw their rivals on the summit start to descend. A few moments later they met Frederic Yeats Browne who with guide was making his first ascent of the season. They exchanged a few words, and Yeats Browne noted that Hadow was, as he put it, fretting to get to the top—and, apparently, 'bent on getting back to Chamonix before us'.

They spent an hour on the summit, waiting for Hudson and M'Cormick and Croz to arrive, and then set off down with all speed. It was still only ten in the morning, but the sun was already beating across the glaring slopes, its rays caught and reflected as in a great bowl, softening the snow so that one went down in it up to the knees. Experience was needed, and this was the one thing Hadow lacked. He was soon falling about and, according to Yeats Browne who looked back more than once at the party behind him, 'kept floundering into crevasses and having to be hauled out again.' Kennedy unroped and went on ahead, apparently to help 'break the trail', while Peter Perren kept Hadow on the tight rope that was necessary. Thus, it was hoped, they could make the best time possible. To Kennedy, 24, and Hadow, 19, it was imperative to show that whatever the 'elderly' Hudson and his friend M'Cormick might do, they could beat all records for the descent.

As it happened, Hudson was not hurrying. He was enjoying himself amid the wonders of the upper world, and more than once he and his friend sat down in the snow and read the Psalms for the day. 'Poor Croz,' comments M'Cormick, 'listened patiently to words he did not understand.'

Below them, their younger companions plunged on at all speed, sliding and jumping down the ice hummocks, Kennedy at one point slipping into a concealed crevasse and pulling himself out only with difficulty. They reached the Pierre Pointue, stopped for only twenty minutes to pay their bill and collect their packs, and kept up the pace down to Chamonix. At three they were back in the Hotel de l'Union, only five hours after they had stood on the summit of Mont Blanc. It was an impressive performance for anyone, let alone an untried 19 year-old making his first big ascent. Both Hudson and M'Cormick, who soberly strolled in a couple of hours later, were more than ready to acknowledge the fact.

That evening they all reviewed their plans. Yeats Browne was there with his friend the Rev. James Robertson, a kindly, round-faced man with a Newgate fringe, a master at Rugby and a future headmaster of Haileybury. With Robertson, Hudson discussed his programme. There was only one item that really mattered of course. But Kennedy was to return to England with his wife the following day; M'Cormick would have to be in Grindelwald the day after that; George Joad might be arriving, but there was really no knowing who might be ready to try the Matterhorn with him next week. Would Robertson like to come? Robertson declined, although he was taking the High Level route to Zermatt with two other masters from Rugby, and would no doubt see Hudson there in a few days' time. He might, of course, change his mind.

The next morning Hudson drove down the valley with Kennedy and his wife, and wished them well on their way. M'Cormick hurried off to Grindelwald, after arranging to meet Hudson at Visp the coming Tuesday, the 11th.

They would then travel together up the Vispthal to Zermatt where M'Cormick was due to officiate on the Sunday. But before then they would have put an end to all argument about the Matterhorn.

After M'Cormick had left, Hudson decided to take things quietly for a few days. He remained in Chamonix for the weekend, then set off with Croz and Hadow for Zermatt. They rested in Martigny, Croz going into one of the local drapers and buying himself a new blue smock of the kind then worn by Savoyards. Then they continued on their way.

They were all quite confident now, Hudson especially, although he had one regret: what a pity that dear good young Kennedy would not be sharing their adventures on the Matterhorn in a few days' time. There was also, it seems likely, one question in his mind.

Where was Edward Whymper?

Whymper lacked the services of Croz. But when he had last been seen, disappearing over the tops with great plans hatching, he had with him Christian Almer, who with Croz and Melchior Anderegg formed the triumvirate of leading Alpine guides. One never knew with Whymper, although he would probably be making the same old mistake of attacking the mountain only from the Italian side. At least, one hoped so. He would be sure to be around somewhere. For even to think of the Matterhorn without Whymper was like thinking of the Mona Lisa without Leonardo, Hamlet without the Prince, or the field of Waterloo without that booted and caped figure of the Duke.

However, God would no doubt decide, and within a few days one would know how things were to turn out.

CHAPTER FOUR

WHYMPER, THE MAN OF THE MATTERHORN

URING THE FIRST DAYS OF JULY, 1865, the Matterhorn was thus pulling towards the valleys which run up to its lower rocks the men who were to play the leading roles in its conquest. Carrel was confident that the great moment for Italy was at hand. Douglas was making his plans with the exuberance of youth while from the foot of Mont Blanc Hudson was travelling with his young companion in the calm assurance that he held a key which would unlock the route to the top.

Meanwhile Edward Whymper, 'the cynosure of all eyes' at Chamonix as Yeats Browne had described him, was busily adding more mountain scalps to his belt, making new ascents, crossing passes for the first time. But in Whymper there burned more brightly than in any of the others that hard gemlike flame consecrated to the Matterhorn. Like Carrel he felt it to be his mountain. Like Carrel, he regarded its conquest as the object of all hope and endeavour. Like Carrel he had risked much on its slopes. As the July days passed he moved, for the second time in as many weeks, towards the Matterhorn. No man was more certain to be in at the kill.

In the summer of 1865 Edward Whymper was in his 26th year. He was tall, and built on a massive scale. His powerful frame concealed a nimbleness on difficult rocks, and his ability to move at a steady five miles an hour, up hill and down dale, had helped in building up his long

Edward Whymper in 1865 at the age of 25

list of mountaineering achievements. In these physical attributes, Whymper had much in common with most contemporary mountaineers.

They were all hard-goers, delighting in brisk exercise, and their successes are only partly qualified by the fact that they moved largely free of loads, with their porters and guides carrying the packs, blankets and impedimenta. As Leslie Stephen, 'fleetest of foot of the whole Alpine fraternity', once put it: 'I do not myself ever cut steps when I can get a guide to do it for me, first because guides can do it very much better; and secondly because he is paid to do it.'

However, Whymper was different from the men whom he met in Seiler's Monte Rosa or the Hotel de l'Union at Chamonix—the scientists and clergymen with whom he corresponded about the qualities of guides; the well-to-do businessmen thrown up by the bubbling cauldron of Victorian industry and commerce to whom the Alps offered a delightful escape from the heavy daily round of work. While most of them had been born into a middle class society, or had already scrambled up into it, Whymper was still on the ladder that led from humble beginnings. He climbed mountains, moreover, for reasons that were not theirs. Neither of these things, alone, would have been important. Together, they would not be important today. But in an age when mountaineering was still frequently justified by appeal to scientific or philosophical motives, when class barriers presented less easily surmounted hurdles than they do today, these things combined to set Edward Whymper apart from the other Englishmen with whom he moved and climbed. It is hardly surprising that the chip on his shoulder was more apparent even than the coil of rope.

Whymper's father, Josiah, the son of an Ipswich brewer, had walked to London in search of fame and fortune with only a few shillings in his pocket; made an improvident marriage; and fathered eleven children of which Edward was the second. Ability had triumphed over adversity as well as the handicap of a numerous family, and by the time of Edward's birth he was already a notable engraver. He had also founded the Lambeth business of book illustrating which his second son was to manage with great skill until the spread of improved photographic processes drove the older craft from the market. Edward had entered the family business somewhat grudgingly, since he would have preferred to train as an engineer, an idea which was firmly put in its place. It is possible that he might have exploited his considerable abilities either thus or in science. Instead, he soon found that he had inherited his father's skill, and by the age of 20 was established as a pillar of the business.

During the summer of 1860 the young Whymper planned to make an extensive business tour of the Continent. Shortly before his departure, the firm was approached by William Longman who with his brother ran the publishing business of Longmans, Green. The firm had four years previously published Hudson and Kennedy's *Ascent of Mont Blanc Without Guides,* the account of their remarkable climb. Longman himself was an original member of the Alpine Club, had published under the title of *Peaks, Passes and Glaciers,* the first series of papers by the Club's members, and now required illustrations for a second volume. Would Mr. Whymper care to provide these?

Whymper agreed—and was thus set upon the path which was to lead him to the Matterhorn.

On his assignment he first visited the Oberland, then travelled to the Valais where at the Zermatt dinner table he found: 'Alpine men, very plucky fellows, the talk continually interesting.' He gladly accepted the offer of Thomas Woodbine Hinchliff to teach him the rudiments of mountaineering. Proceeding without hurry eastwards across Switzerland, he reached the Dauphiné, made his sketches, and returned to England. He had, he later wrote, acquired a 'passion for mountain scrambling' and he planned to return to the Alps the following year. Two peaks in particular attracted him, the Weisshorn and the Matterhorn, both unclimbed. And his attitude to mountaineering was epitomised by his comment when he heard of Tyndall's success on the Weisshorn—his 'interest in the Weisshorn abated, but it was raised to the highest pitch on hearing that Professor Tyndall was at Breuil, and intending to try to crown his first victory by another and still greater one.'

It was not, of course, so very reprehensible to regard mountaineering as a field of personal rivalry. All the great climbers of the day sought their 'firsts' with vigour and determination. One difference with Whymper—which, human nature being what it is, may well have lost him friends—was that he was more vigorous and more determined than the rest. It was not the only difference, however. Whymper invariably lost interest in a mountain once it had been climbed. To be first was the great affair. Most others buttressed the pleasures of gaining a 'first' with enjoyment of the struggle for its own sake, knowing that no mountain is ever twice the same, delighting in the wonders of the upper world, forgetting their business worries, working off the surplus carbohydrates, content that all this should be really part of a great game which would, alas, end after six weeks or so. Such men were summarised a few decades later by Godley for whom the climber was the man

> Leaving England far astern
> With a ticket through to Bern,
> And regarding [his] profession with a lordly unconcern.

He was the man who could gladly claim that

> Any mountains will content me, though they've all been climbed before—
> Yes! I care not any more
> Though they've all been done before,
> And the names they keep in bottles may be numbered by the score!

Whymper was made of other stuff, and the intensity with which he fought the mountain battle tended to cut him off from his contemporaries. They might regard it as a sport in which, most of them well knew, they were the amateurs and the guides were the professionals. Whymper must have seemed to many of them to ignore this convenient boundary, bringing to the pleasant pastime a ruthless efficiency which was, somehow, not quite the thing.

He was also in one sense a professional mountaineer himself. His introduction to the Alps had been, after all, a business venture. He continued to sketch, not as a hobby, but actually so that he could illustrate books with pictures of the Alps! He was, when one stopped to think about it, almost an employee of Mr. Longman. None of this would have counted for so much had he not been so successful. That was, perhaps, the most galling thing of all.

Only on the Matterhorn did Whymper appear to meet his match. He had first seen the mountain when coming up the Vispthal to Zermatt, and the sight failed to inspire him. 'It may be compared to a sugar loaf set up on a table; the sugar loaf should have its head knocked on one side,' he wrote in his diary. 'Grand it is, but beautiful I think it is not.' A decade later, writing for publication, his views had changed. 'Ages hence, generations unborn will gaze upon its awful precipices and wonder at its unique form' he declaimed. 'However exalted may be their ideas, and however exaggerated their expectations, none will come to return disappointed.' It would be unfair to claim that this *volte-face* was accounted for solely by salesmanship, by a desire to tell a good tale. Mountains are physically shaped by the elements, but the impact which they make on the human mind depends largely on their human associations and the parts they have played in human lives. By 1870 the Matterhorn had played many parts and had been changed by human endeavour. So, too, had Edward Whymper. When in 1860 he had seen it from Zermatt 'the eastern face . . . seemed one smooth, inaccessible cliff from summit to base' while from Breuil 'the mountain is seen to be broken up into a series of pyramidical wedge-shaped masses.' When he returned the following year, he had therefore gone to the southern side—writing in the guest book of one Alpine inn, 'Edward Whymper, *en-route* for the Matterhorn'. He had experienced his first brush with Carrel, and climbed up the Italian ridge to a height of about 12,650 feet before being stopped by the temerity of his Oberland guide who refused to go higher. It was possibly this humiliating setback when, as he put it, he 'had to eat humble pie', that helped to force him into the activity of the next year—a year in which he made four separate attempts to climb the mountain from Breuil.

These prolonged assaults of July 1862 were testimony to Whymper's aggressive determination and to the practical way in which he tackled mountaineering problems. He had no inhibitions about what would now be called 'mechanical aids', looked on the use of metal pitons as the most natural thing in the world, and even devised a special 'claw' as he called it. This was a double-pronged affair, and was attached to a length of rope through a hole where the two prongs met. On the mountain it could be pulled from the rucksack at the foot of what might have been an impassable stretch of rock and hurled up until the claw eventually caught on a rock; then the rope could be used over an otherwise holdless stretch. There were other 'tools of suspicious appearance', as Whymper called them. There were, at least in 1863 and possibly even earlier, 'two ladders, each twelve feet long, which joined together like those used by firemen, and shut up like parallel rulers.' There was also the Whymper Tent, as it became known, an ingeniously-designed piece of equipment considerably in advance of anything else then available.

In 1862, Whymper's first two attempts on the Matterhorn were made with Reginald Macdonald, a clerk in the Colonial Office of the same age as himself. The two men met at Zermatt early in July, crossed the Théodule to Breuil, and a few days later camped out on the Col du Lion. Here, with the Italian ridge soaring away above them, they were pinned down by bad weather. They succeeded in getting only 100ft up from the Col before the wind became too much for them. 'Advance or return was alike impossible,' wrote Whymper later, 'the ridge was denuded of its debris; and we clutched our hardest when we saw stones as big as a man's fist blown away horizontally into space.' Clinging to the rocks, moving at times on all fours, they eventually got back to the Col, and their two Zermatt guides decided that they had had enough.

The whole party retreated to Breuil where, almost inevitably it must have seemed, Jean-Antoine Carrel had arrived—suspicious now that the English were once more reconnoitring his mountain. He agreed to go with them on the first fine day—but only if the party were accompanied by a second guide. The weather improved more quickly than Whymper had any right to expect and the following day they set off once again. This time they pushed on for some hundred feet above the Col du Lion

'A cannonade on the Matterhorn (1862)' —one of Whymper's illustrations from Scrambles

before deciding to camp, reconnoitred the ridge above, then returned to spend the night in the tent. All looked promising. The weather was good and at 5.15am the following morning they were off. Carrel, Whymper and Macdonald scrambled up the Chimney. So did the second guide. But when he emerged at the top of the pitch he declared that he could go no further.

That, so far as Carrel was concerned, settled the matter. He would not go on alone. Once again Whymper and Macdonald were forced to retreat. Once more they returned to Breuil—and this time Macdonald was reluctantly forced to leave for home.

Whymper had been stopped not by any inability of his own, nor even by the excessive difficulty of the rocks. The weather and the guides, those were the things, and he probably complained in his energetic way as he crossed the Théodule once more to Zermatt in the hope of finding another guide there. Instead, he had to put up with a week of storms.

Yet a third time he crossed the Théodule, and decided to make a solitary trip to the platform above the Col du Lion, where he had left his tent for future use. By now the weather had changed. The conditions were perfect, and he watched the sun go down and the moon slowly rise over a scene so silent that 'the world seemed dead, and I its sole inhabitant'.

If anything further was needed to concentrate Whymper's attention on the Matterhorn, and to transform an interest into an obsession, it was that night alone on the Italian ridge. He sat for some time at the door of the tent and eight years later remembered one sight above all others. 'Something in the south hung like a great glowworm in the air,' he wrote, 'it was too large for a star, and too steady for a meteor; and it was long before I could realise the scarcely credible fact that it was the moonlight glittering on the great snow slope on the north side of Monte Viso, at a distance, as the crow flies, of 98 miles.'

Next morning he set off upwards alone, along the unknown ridge, determined to press on until physically stopped by the difficulty of the rocks. At places he was helped by the 'claw'. At others he climbed unaided, watching the other peaks of the Pennines gradually sink beneath him. He passed the previous difficulties. He passed the place where Carrel had carved out his sign of ownership. He pushed on until, eventually, the rocks were too much for him and he saw that he would soon be brought to a halt. But he had reached about 13,400ft—higher than anyone had ever gone on the Matterhorn. Even today, when the limits of the possible have been extended, it would have been a daring exploit for a man of Whymper's slight experience. For Whymper it was a *tour de force*. It also nearly cost him his life.

Whymper's drawing of the tent platform on the Col du Lion, from Scrambles

He descended to the tent platform in safety and left the tent in position, quite confident now that on his return he would, with support, be able to go on to the top. Then he went down to the Col du Lion and began the descent to the easier ground on to which the rock slopes led.

It was in negotiating a tricky corner that he slipped and fell. He pitched into some rocks a dozen feet below, and rebounded into a gully. 'I whirled downwards in a series of bounds, each longer than the last,' he later wrote, 'now over ice, now into rocks; striking my head four or five times, each time with increased force. The last bound sent me spinning through the air, in a leap of fifty or sixty feet, from one side of the gully to the other, and I struck the rocks, luckily, with the whole of my left side. They caught my clothes for a moment, and I fell back on to the snow with motion arrested.' He had fallen nearly 200 feet in seven or eight bounds; the next one would have taken him 800 feet on to the glacier below.

With blood spurting from a multiplicity of wounds, he fainted. When he regained consciousness the sun was setting, and it was dark long before he was off the rocks. Yet he descended the 4,900ft to Breuil without further slip—an example of that iron self control which was to isolate him from most other men. The accident was also to play a vital part in events three summers later. For as Whymper lay at Breuil recovering—the speed of this being, he later believed, due to the local treatment of rubbing a mixture of hot wine and salt into the wounds—he made a vow that 'if any Englishman should at any time fall sick in the Valtournanche he should not feel so solitary as I did at this dreary time.'

He had fallen on the 19th. Only four days later he set out from Breuil again, this time with Jean-Antoine Carrel, who had been brought up by news of the accident, and by Caesar Carrel. They got high on the mountain but not as high as Whymper had gone alone. Once again, the weather broke. Whymper was all for staying and awaiting a change; the two guides insisted on returning, and return they did. There seems little doubt of the cause. Whymper was never uncharitable in his opinion of Carrel—as he was of many others—but even he had to say that although Carrel 'wished very much to be the first man on the top, and did not object to be accompanied by anyone else who had the same wish, he had no intention of letting one succeed too soon—perhaps to give a greater appearance of *éclat* when the thing was accomplished.'

Whymper made one more attempt that season, going up to the tent platform with a porter, since the Carrels now claimed to be occupied with other business. This time he failed to get as far as before up the now familiar cliffs. And he returned to find that Professor Tyndall, the conqueror of the Weisshorn, had arrived at Breuil, had engaged Carrel to support his own Swiss guide, and was to start the following morning. But Tyndall had engaged Carrel only as a porter—a fact that was to have its effect when, high on the mountain, Tyndall appealed to Carrel's local knowledge. Jean-Antoine Carrel replied that he and his cousin had been engaged merely as porters. Tyndall, like Whymper before him, was brought to a halt, even though he reached more than 13,900ft, less than a thousand feet from the summit.

By the end of 1862 the Matterhorn had thus repulsed both Professor Tyndall, one of the finest mountaineers of his day, and Edward Whymper who had made no less than five separate attempts to climb it. Like Everest more than half a century later, its ascent appeared to demand a special combination of factors. The men had to be technically capable. The guides had to be willing. The weather had to contribute by giving a good period long enough to clear the upper slopes of excess snow and then to enable men to fight a way towards the summit. Yet when all these factors had been satisfied, who knew that there did not lie, somewhere on the last 1,000ft, some stretch that would bar the most daring invader. As Whymper himself put it, a completely holdless rock of little more than seven feet would be enough to stop anyone if it were vertical and if it completely barred the way.

Yet in spite of the discouragements Whymper came back for more punishment the following year. He was the only one who did. But in the August of 1863 he came up to Breuil, hired the two Carrels and three porters, and set out on his most ambitious attempt. Once again, he was unable to press up even to the point he had reached on his lone assault.

This time the rocks were iced or under snow. A frightening thunder-storm broke around the party. And eventually even the persistent Whymper was forced down, with his heavy baggage, his tent and blankets, his provisions, ladder, and some 450 feet of rope. 'I arrived at Châtillon at midnight on the 11th defeated and disconsolate' he later wrote, 'but, like a gambler who loses each throw, only the more eager to have another try, to see if the luck would change; and returned to London ready to devise fresh combinations, and to form new plans.'

These plans matured the following year, a year in which Whymper rose to the peak of his performance as an audacious mountaineer. First, with A. W. Moore and Horace Walker, he made a spirited journey across the Dauphiné, crossing the Breche de la Meije for the first time and making the first ascent of the Ecrins, the highest peak in the group. Then he struck back east towards Mont Blanc and within a week had secured three more gratifying 'firsts'—Mont Dolent, the Aiguille de Trélatête, and the Aiguille d'Argentière.

These last three mountains were climbed with Anthony Adams-Reilly, like Whymper an artist of ability and the man who the previous year had prepared from his own survey figures the first accurate map of the Mont Blanc range. The two men parted after the ascent of the Aiguille d'Argentière and arranged to meet in Zermatt four days later. Reilly was 'convoying stores' in Whymper's words, and from what we know it seems likely that a major siege of the Matterhorn was contemplated. This time, however, yet another misfortune was to stop the operations before they had started. At Zermatt Whymper collected his mail from the post of-fice. It brought, as he put it, 'disastrous intelligence', which appears to have been of a business nature. He waited for Reilly, who entered Zermatt only to learn that his friend had to leave for England immediately. It was already mid-July, and all thought of a further attack on the Matterhorn that year had to be abandoned.

Thus Whymper came to 1865. 'Our career in 1864 had been one of unbroken success, but the great ascent upon which I had set my heart was not attempted, and, until it was accomplished, I was unsatisfied', he wrote. By this time he had, moreover, conceived a new scheme. In his numerous sorties around the mountain he had at last begun to suspect that the apparent difficulties of the great eastern face might be something of an illusion. Strangely, perhaps, he was drawn to this rather than to the northern ridge which bounded it and it was the eastern face on which he had his eye when he arrived at Zermatt the following year. His guides were Christian Almer, Franz Biener—who appears to have acted more as a porter than as a guide—and Michel Croz with whom he had carried out so many famous ascents.

Croz was his favourite, one of the few guides from whom he did not exact the most strict master-and-servant discipline. He was a man, like Whymper, greedy of mountain success. 'He did not work like a blunt razor, and take to his toil unkindly', Whymper wrote of him. 'He did not need urging, or to be told a second time to do anything. You had only to say *what* was to be done, and *how* it was to be done, and the work *was* done, if it was possible.'

At the end of the 1864 season Whymper had engaged him for the following year. But the misunderstanding by which Croz had become engaged by Birkbeck had disrupted his plans. Any climbs with Croz, on the Matterhorn or elsewhere, would have to be finished by June 27th.

There was a further complication. 'When it came to the point, neither Croz nor Almer were persuaded by Whymper's opinion of the east face. A compromise was arranged, and the party made the ascent of the Théodulhorn, above the Théodule Pass, to study the rocks from as close as possible. One can envisage them from this vantage point looking up the south-east, or Furggen ridge, which led to the summit. On the right of the ridge stretches the east face; on the left lie the broken precipices on the southern side of the mountain. Whymper and his guides now noticed a deep gully running up to a point high on the south-east ridge. Why not, they argued, climb this gully to the ridge and then cross over on to the east face high up, traverse it on to the north ridge, and thence make for the summit by the best available route?

They tried this the following day, making an attempt which, in Arnold

Michel Croz

Lunn's words, was 'a classic example of the fallibility of experts, for the most inexperienced of novices could hardly have picked a worse route'. They reached the foot of the gully without difficulty, only to find it swept by falling stones which ricocheted down and across it like gunfire. The rocks beside the gully proved impracticable.

"Why don't you try to go up a mountain which can be ascended?" Almer asked.

And at Whymper's suggestion that they should cross back to the Zermatt side to tackle the eastern face after all, Croz reminded him of his engagement in a week's time. Whymper recorded the exact words in *Scrambles*.

"Sir," Croz said, "if we cross to the other side we shall lose three days, and very likely shall not succeed. You want to make ascents in the chain of Mont Blanc, and I believe they can be made. But I shall not be able to make them with you if I spend these days here, for I must be at Chamonix on the 27th."

Therefore they went down to Breuil. They left Breuil for Chamonix, making en route the first ascent of the western summit of the Grandes Jorasses and the first passage of the Col Dolent. And they arrived in Chamonix at 10pm on the night of 26th. Croz was in time for Birkbeck, for whom he waited while Whymper went off for the Aiguille Verte with Almer and Biener.

That 'first'—a very fine specimen—safely tucked away, Whymper could now turn to more serious matters. One possibility offered itself. He would make a new glacier pass across the Mont Blanc massif to Courmayeur. Thence he could take the carriage down to Aosta, and so, once more, up the Valtournanche for the Matterhorn.

Whymper now looked about him. It has often been stated that he was an unfriendly man. It is certainly true that in later life he developed a certain rugged aggressiveness towards much of mankind that had some kinship with the mountain he had so much coveted. Yet at times he demonstrated a surprising friendly sociability. This was one of them, and he turned to another Englishman, the Rev. A. G. Girdlestone, who, like Hudson, was one of the muscular Christians by this time assaulting the Alps in increasing numbers. Girdlestone had left London with a friend he wished to introduce to the mountains. The introduction proved too fierce, and the companion was soon making his way back to England leaving his mentor to cope alone with his 17-year-old pupil, Walter Hargreaves. He was an adventurous, if at this time relatively inexperienced mountaineer, and Whymper appears to have warmed to him as a man after his own heart. Later, when his account of guideless climbing, and the recklessness it indicated, affronted the common sense of the Alpine Club, Whymper's attitude changed. Now he was all friendliness.

Would Girdlestone and young Hargreaves like to join him in making a new route to Courmayeur? Girdlestone declined—ostensibly on the grounds that he wished to see the finer, but well known and easier, Col du Geant; in reality, it seems likely, because he shied from the thought of linking an untried 17-year-old to Whymper's experience.

However, they went up to the Montenvers and set out together the following morning. Then Whymper swung away eastwards for what was to be the first crossing of the Col de Tâlèfre. He was down in Courmayeur by the late afternoon, while it was 8.30pm before Girdlestone and Hargreaves arrived from the far easier expedition.

The following morning they left together once again, taking the carriage to Villeneuve where Girdlestone and Hargreaves got down for the walk up to Cogne, whence they hoped to ascend the Grivola. Whymper drove on to Aosta. Then he made for the old magnet, the Matterhorn. But he did not travel direct. Instead, as he says, they 'took a route across country, and bagged upon our way the summit of the Ruinette'. This, of course, was but putting off the final decision. He could not go on for ever like this. Therefore he now made for Breuil. No doubt Carrel would be available.

Thus on July 7th, 1865, as Hudson and Hadow were ascending Mont Blanc, Lord Francis Douglas traversing the Ober Gabelhorn from Zinal to Zermatt, and Carrel returning from a reconnaissance of the Matterhorn for his Italian supporters, Whymper and his two guides were cutting their way up a slope towards the Col de Valcournera. Beyond lay the Valtournanche, with the Matterhorn at its head still deep in cloud.

PART TWO

THE PLAY BEGINS

CHAPTER FIVE

PARTIES CONVERGING ON A MOUNTAIN

WHYMPER AND HIS GUIDES KICKED STEPS up the narrowing couloir until, as the rocks closed in on either side, the ground fell away before them and they reached the col. Beyond it, a small glacier sloped down towards a lake at the head of the wild Fontanella glen.

Already a fresh idea was forming in Whymper's mind. There was more than one way of dealing with that particular mountain. You needed more than one way when you had to deal with the obstinacy of some guides. All the way up from Prarayé, he had been trying to persuade them; all the time he received the same answer. Even from Almer, the great Christian Almer, 'the unsurpassed and unsurpassable', who repeated in answer to all entreaties: "*Anything* but Matterhorn, dear sir! *Anything* but Matterhorn!"

It looked as though he would be unable to convince them. But there was no harm in trying to get a second string to his bow, and by the time they reached the head of the Fontanella glen he had made up his mind.

We do not know what he said. But Whymper had no excess of tact, and it seems likely that he merely, as he described it, 'sent them by the short cut to Breuil'. There they would await his arrival and his instructions. But while they moved off north-east, across the little col south of Mont Rouss and then along the grass track to Breuil, he would be making for Valtournanche. Carrel might be there. If so, he could dispense with Almer and Biener; if not, he could make a last effort to shame them into crossing to Zermatt and attempting the Matterhorn from the north.

He watched the men on their way, then followed the stream from the lake, down the steep rocks that led into the Fontanella gorge, down the path past the huts of Cignana, then on to the road only a mile or so below Valtournanche.

Whymper strode into the village and demanded Carrel. The guide was not there, and he had to ask a number of villagers before he found out that Carrel had left the previous day with some of the other men. He was trying, once again, to climb the Matterhorn, and Whymper might have worried but for one thing. The clouds were low down. Even before you reached the serious defences of the Matterhorn you would, on a day like this, be moving almost blind, through a thick blanket, with the water streaming off the rocks, with even the best sense of direction fuddled by the grey envelope, and with cold and discouragement as constant companions.

Yet, unknown to Whymper, there already existed in the village of Valtournanche something that would have caused him bitter worry had he known of it. For Fate was now taking a hand and setting lazily in motion the machinery which was to bring together in one story Carrel and Croz, Lord Francis Douglas and Hadow, Whymper and Hudson. Awaiting Carrel there lay a letter from Giordano. It enclosed 200 francs to cover out-of-pocket expenses and an advance payment. It mentioned a tent, a thousand feet of rope, iron hoops and rings—the forerunners of the modern pitons and karabiners and provisions. All these, more than 200 pounds of them, had been sent by Giordano from Turin to Châtillon. Carrel, the letter said, was to collect them at once and order their movement up to Breuil. At last—the Italians were coming. 'Let us, then,' Giordano was writing to Quintino Sella on this very day, 'let us set out to attack this Devil's mountain, and let us see that we succeed, if only Whymper has not been beforehand with us.'

So far, Carrel knew nothing of this. He knew nothing of it as Whymper, confident that little would happen on the mountain in weather like this, walked past the house where the unopened letter lay.

As usual he was right. He reckoned that Carrel would be on his way

Two views of the Hornli Ridge—(right) viewed from Zermatt and (above) in profile showing the true angle of the ridge

back, that he would meet the guide on the track to Breuil. Halfway there he saw a group of men clustered round a chalet on the far side of the stream. He splashed across to them and found Jean-Antoine and Caesar Carrel, Aimé Gorret and Jean-Joseph Maquignaz, all commiserating among themselves on the appalling weather. They had only just been able to reach the Glacier du Lion.

Whymper came quickly to the point. He explained that he believed the east face of the Matterhorn to be less steep than had always been supposed. There, he argued with Carrel, lay the key to success that they had all been too stupid to see. If you were going to climb the Matterhorn from the Italian side you first had to cross the Théodule, and they should do just that. Carrel and another man should come up the following day to Breuil. They could cross the pass by moonlight and spend the whole of the 10th getting as high as possible on the east face. They could pitch their tent there—and on the 11th victory would be theirs.

It was all very attractive. Except to Carrel. For to Carrel it was essential not only that he should be first on the top of the mountain, but that the ascent should be made directly by the Italian route, from his own valley, without that crossing of the frontier, without the use of a route that would give half the laurels to the Swiss, as well as most of the future business. It was a natural enough reaction; there was no bitterness about it; and if international rivalry and pride went no further the world would be a less dangerous place.

Yet if he rejected Whymper's proposal, what then? There would be nothing to prevent the Englishman from crossing into Switzerland, picking up what guides he could, and trying direct from Zermatt. The Italian version of the saying about half a loaf being better than no bread passed through Carrel's mind. He would settle for a compromise: he would come up to Breuil in two days' time, on Sunday the 9th, and they would cross the Théodule and make the attempt that Whymper suggested. But if they failed they would return to Breuil and make yet another effort on the Italian ridge they both knew so well.

The Englishman and the Italians parted, Whymper striding uphill to Breuil, the others going down to Valtournanche, starting that confusing up-and-down traffic which within the next few days was to complicate the unfolding history of the Matterhorn.

Whymper reached Breuil and continued on upwards past the huts to Favre's little inn on the Jomein. Here he found Almer and Biener waiting as ordered. He discharged them—'with much regret, for no two men ever served me more faithfully or more willingly' as he later recorded. Nevertheless, they obviously had no heart for the Matterhorn venture and would be better out of it. Whymper must have gone to bed that Friday evening quite confident.

Saturday was stormy. The clouds were still low down, and there seemed little sign of any break as Almer and Biener shook hands with their employer and moved up the track towards the Théodule which lay somewhere above in the mist.

There was plenty to be done. Carrel and two others would be coming up the following day, Whymper explained to Favre, and they would need provisions for at least two days. He checked the ropes and his tent, unrolling the six-foot-six ash poles from the unbleached calico, looking over cords, seams, fastenings. He probably regretted more than once that Carrel would not be coming up that afternoon, even though the weather was still bad. They might at least have crossed the Théodule and taken up a position from which they could quickly exploit any lifting of the clouds. Had they done so, history would have been very different.

That evening, as Whymper sat restlessly waiting, a figure was seen making up from the huts of Breuil. The man was alone, and was travelling fast. As he came nearer, Whymper thought that he was vaguely familiar. Then, through his glass, he recognised Walter Hargreaves.

As they sat outside the hotel a few minutes later, Hargreaves explained how illness had intervened; how Girdlestone had barely managed to reach Cogne; how they had abandoned any idea of an ascent of the Grivola, turned back on their tracks, and had intended to cross the Théodule to Zermatt. His companion had struggled up to Valtournanche. He could go no farther; but he had sent on Hargreaves whose father would be waiting in Zermatt.

It was an unfortunate tale. And as it unwound Whymper, forever a man of his word, remembered the vow he had made three years previously—'that if an Englishman should at any time fall sick in the Val Tournanche he should not feel so solitary as I did . . .'

Here was the Englishman. It was annoying, of course. It might even wreck one's plans for the Matterhorn. But one's word was one's word.

After breakfast the following morning, Sunday July 9th, Whymper set off down the path from the Jomein.

He had passed the houses of Breuil when he saw a miniature caravan winding up from Valtournanche. At its head was someone whom Whymper recognised only as 'a foreign gentleman'. It was in fact Felice Giordano. Behind Giordano came a mule, several porters and guides. All were heavily laden, for in addition to the supplies which Giordano had sent on ahead for collection at Châtillon he himself had arrived with an extra tent and with no less than three barometers, two of which were now being carried by Jean-Antoine and Caesar Carrel.

Whymper was surprised. But as yet he was not alarmed. Carrel, after all, would be serving him from that evening and he asked what he and Caesar were doing. He was told that the foreigner had arrived just as the Carrels were setting out, and that they were helping his porters.

This was a fiddling with the truth that Jean-Antoine thought was justified by the situation. For he had arrived home on the Friday evening to learn that Giordano was at last coming. He had travelled down to Châtillon on the Saturday, conducted his client up to the village of Valtournanche, and had been impressed by the massive scale of the operation which the Italians were mounting. He, too, now had a double string to his bow. For he could, hand on heart, try with Whymper if the weather quickly cleared; if not, the siege tactics of Giordano surely could not fail.

But he now had to explain to Whymper that Tuesday was the last day on which he would be available. For by then Giordano's preparations would be complete on the Italian side of the mountain. So he explained that he was, as he put it, engaged to travel "with a family of distinction". As was the case with most of his important encounters with Carrel, Whymper meticulously recorded the exact words used—and it is difficult not to feel that he did so largely in fairness to the guide.

"And Caesar also?" he queried.

"And Caesar also."

"Why did you not say this before?" Whymper demanded.

"Because", came the truthful reply, "it was not settled. The engagement is of long standing, but the day was not fixed. When I got back to Valtournanche on Friday night, after leaving you, I found a letter naming the day."

One can hardly blame Carrel. He did not state that the tall man striding on ahead of him while he and Whymper talked was in fact the man he hoped to lead to the top of the Matterhorn. He did not hint that, with the weather still bad, the chances were growing that he might be able to snatch an Italian victory from beneath Whymper's nose. Indeed, why should he? He was a free man, who had decided that from the Sunday evening he would put himself at the disposal of the foreigner. He would do so honestly—and at the end of his employment he would work as well for the next man. Like a good soldier in Housman's army of mercenaries he would, whenever the Heavens were falling, save the sum of things for pay. But in the weighing of personal and national loyalties there seemed no need to tell Whymper of the way the battle might be going. Whymper, years later, when he had learned at least some of the facts, admitted as much. 'I could not object to the answer', he wrote of Carrel's reply.

The two men parted, Carrel hurrying on to catch up with Giordano, Whymper turning down towards the campanile of Valtournanche, hoping that the weather had not closed in for good, wondering if he dare hope that it might have lifted by evening. For there was now no time left for accidents. Either they would leave that night, camp out high on Monday, and try for the summit on Tuesday, or he might as well abandon the attempt. The Matterhorn was hardly a mountain on which you could squeeze three days' efforts into two.

However, there might still be time enough. It was early as Whymper walked into the inn and asked for Girdlestone. It was an unpretentious place which within a few years had been raised from 'the most miserable of hotels' as one traveller called it, to 'homely but clean and cheap'—for a place of this sort the highest praise that a writer of guidebooks could give. Only a few years ago the beds had been mere berths in the corners of the small room that did service as dining room. Now, with its blue-flowered wallpaper, and painted plaster cats on the chimneypiece, it was dining room alone, and Whymper was led up narrow stairs to the room, almost as narrow, where Girdlestone lay ill in bed.

The clergyman was surprised by his visitor. He was really quite better, he insisted—tumbling out on to the floor in a fainting fit at the same moment.

To Whymper it was quite clear that the man needed medicine, and there was none in Valtournanche. The nearest place where there was any chance of getting what he needed was Châtillon, down in the Aosta Valley. It was typical of Whymper that he gave little thought to the journey—ten miles at a swinging touch-and-pass pace down the valley and then ten miles back through worsening conditions, with the rain sheeting down, and an uphill pull of 3,000 feet. But the weather had been good when he had started, and Girdlestone was under no illusions. 'Such acts from a mountaineer, in glorious weather, showed an unselfishness only to be appreciated by those who know the feeling of giving up a fine day or two which perhaps may not be had again for weeks', he wrote in a letter home. The point seems worth making—enough were to be made on the other side of Whymper's ledger in the years to come.

By the time Whymper had reached Châtillon, sought out the apothecary, explained in his poor French exactly what he wanted, and made his way up the valley once again, it was almost dark. Above the last steep rise into the hamlet itself he reached the church porch in the gathering gloom and saw a figure about to pass him.

He shouted an enquiry and in reply heard a familiar voice: "Jean-Antoine." Once again he has left us an account of exactly what was said.

"I thought you were up at Breuil", he commented with some annoyance.

"No, sir," Carrel explained. "When the storms came on I knew we should not start tonight, and so came down to sleep here."

"Ha, Carrel," Whymper answered, "that is a great bore. If tomorrow is not fine we shall not be able to do anything together. I have sent away my guides, relying on you; and now you are going to leave me to travel with a party of ladies. That work is not fit for you."

In the half-darkness, Whymper thought that he saw a smile on Carrel's face. He could understand it. The man would be pleased to know that the Englishman realised that such work—'carrying a shawl for the ladies across the glacier', as one guide had contemptuously termed it—

was far beneath him. Carrel, much as he respected Whymper, was smiling for another reason.

"Can't you send someone else?" he was asked.

"No, monsieur", he replied. "I am sorry, but my word is pledged. I should like to accompany you, but I can't break my engagement."

They had been walking as they talked, and by this time had reached the door of the inn.

"Well, it is no fault of yours", Whymper concluded. "Come presently with Caesar and have some wine."

He went inside and up to Girdlestone, and insisted that he swallowed a first strong dose of the medicine. Then, since his own things were up at Breuil, he borrowed some from Girdlestone and went downstairs for food.

The two guides came in soon afterwards, and over the glasses they talked of their past adventures. No doubt they talked of how one day the Matterhorn would be climbed. But neither Jean-Antoine nor Caesar revealed that a few miles farther up the valley, above Breuil and above the Jomein, porters were already making a cache of Giordano's provisions, ropes, hammers and other equipment; a cache as high up under the mountain as possible, so that everything could be put into the attack as soon as conditions were right.

They sat up drinking until midnight. There was, after all, no cause for hurry. The following morning, Monday, Whymper looked out of the window to see just what had been expected. The grey clouds still covered the lower slopes and Girdlestone commiserated with him. Shortly afterwards, a group of more than a dozen tourists passed through Valtournanche, bound for Breuil. As Girdlestone wrote home, 'Whymper went ahead and reserved a quiet bed for me as there were only ten bedrooms and several people already there'. He was by this time responding to the rough-and-ready treatment, and would follow at something less than Whymper's breakneck pace.

Halfway up to Breuil Whymper saw the two Carrels once again hovering round the chalet on the far side of the river. He went across to them and bade them goodbye. It might, after all, be the last he would be seeing of them this year; they were, whatever else happened, good friends who had stood together in dangerous places, linked by the bond which unites men who have together survived such experiences.

When Whymper arrived back at the Jomein, the tourists had passed on and he found the inn almost empty. Its sole occupant was Giordano, still quietly nursing his knowledge. So far as information was concerned, he stood on the higher ground, for although Whymper had no suspicions of him, he himself was well aware of Whymper's record and of his ambitions. 'I have tried to keep everything secret,' he wrote to Sella, 'but that fellow, whose life seems to depend on the Matterhorn, is here, suspiciously prying into everything. I have taken all the competent men away from him, and yet he is so enamoured of this mountain that he may go up with others and make a scene. He is here, in this hotel, and I try to avoid speaking to him.'

It was a wretched Monday, with Giordano anxious for a turn in the weather, Whymper filling in time, and kicking his heels while he waited for Girdlestone to come up and be piloted across the Théodule to Zermatt. There was not even the tourist traffic from Zermatt, since the bad weather had discouraged visitors from venturing up with their guides and gaining, by the passage of the pass, a glimpse into the upper mountain world at the cost of little difficulty and less danger.

That evening, in Whymper's words, Girdlestone 'crawled up, a good deal better'.

He came with the luggage with which he was travelling the Continent, and judging by the recommendations which he later made to others this was extensive. In addition to ordinary changes of clothing, the mountain wanderer should, he advised, have a large black leather bag, 'rope, belt, strong lace-boots, one pair of spare laces, boating shoes, mountain gloves, dark spectacles, veil, opera glasses, cold cream, calendula, diachylon, lint bandage, medicine, tea, Liebig's extract, pocket-flask and cup, string, needles and metal matchbox, compass, maps, guidebooks, gaiters, comforter, waterproof, straw hat, light spare shirt', and of course knapsack and ice axe or alpenstock. The items on this list—to which Girdlestone added umbrella with a query beside it—enabled him to move about virtually self-supporting for all except basic food and drink; and its bulk, weight and inconvenience was much mitigated by the fact that the cost of a tour made with it—fifteen weeks for £100—included the hire of porters and mules as necessary.

Girdlestone was the only arrival at the Jomein on the Monday. He chatted for a while with Whymper and then the two men decided to turn in, Whymper's frustration mitigated only by the fact that if the weather kept him from the Matterhorn it would keep all others.

Later that evening, the clouds began to lift. The Matterhorn itself was still shrouded, but the mists which had covered even the meadows leading up to the Théodule slowly began to disperse.

Down in Valtournanche, the Carrels metaphorically sniffed the weather. A change was coming. Jean-Antoine and Caesar decided that the time had arrived. They collected their ropes and equipment, and marched up the track to Breuil, under a sky through which a few stars were raggedly beginning to show.

At the Jomein they roused Giordano. They would take up the tents, they told him, camp out as high as they could, and reconnoitre the upper parts of the route, those rock walls and battlements through which they had yet to find a way.

Giordano was all for going with them. They dissuaded him. When they were confident of success they would send for him; until then he would have to contain his patience at the Jomein.

They discussed their plans. They parcelled out the tents and the equipment between the five porters from Valtournanche and from Breuil whom they had paid to hold themselves ready for just such an occasion. And in the early hours of July 11th the two Carrels and their porters set out across the Alpine meadows for the upper huts of Avouil, where the bulk of their equipment was already cached.

Meanwhile Whymper slept on unsuspectingly.

Girdlestone was up first that morning, going downstairs to smile at the better weather, and then being told by a satisfied Favre that the Italians were now out in strength upon the Matterhorn.

A few moments later he was in Whymper's room, asking whether he had heard the news.

"No. What news?" Whymper sleepily replied.

"Why," he was told, "a large party of guides went off this morning to try the Matterhorn, taking with them a mule laden with provisions."

At first, Whymper hardly believed it. Then, quickly slipping on trousers and shirt, he ran downstairs, telescope in hand.

From the door, in the clear morning light, he could see clearly in the small round circle of his glass the unmistakable black figures moving slowly across the lower slopes of the mountain beneath the towering wall of precipices that fall from the Italian ridge.

Favre stood nearby, watching with a combination of national pride, financial anticipation and the satisfaction that comes of being the supporter of the winning side in a hard-fought contest. Yet again, Whymper underlined his relations with Carrel by quoting the conversation as he remembered it.

"What is all this about?" he demanded. "Who is the leader of this party?"

"Carrel," Favre replied.

"What, Jean-Antoine?"

"Yes; Jean-Antoine."

"Is Caesar there, too?"

"Yes, he is there," Favre answered.

Whymper's reaction was natural enough. He felt that he had been 'bamboozled and humbugged'. The words are significant, for even in the moment of revelation Whymper could not claim that Carrel or Favre or anyone else for that matter, had acted treacherously, told him lies—or perhaps even gone beyond that practice of interpreting the rules to one's own advantage which is a common feature of human relationships. That, of course, made it all the harder to bear. For four years he had thought and dreamed of the Matterhorn. He had made seven attempts to climb it, pushing chance and good luck until they could be pushed no farther. He had been high on the mountain as many times as Carrel; only one party, Tyndall's of three years ago, had been higher. Now, unless Fate played some unexpected cards, he would be left below the snowline, and with a good view of his rivals reaching the summit.

Whymper quickly learned what had happened. Now that the secret was out, Favre was only too glad to tell him how a reconnaissance had been made the previous week, how vast quantities of provisions, huge lengths of rope, and much special equipment had already been taken up to the lower slopes for the attempt.

Girdlestone had too little experience to be of help. But something must be done. Whymper went up to his room and was soon enveloped in clouds of smoke from the dark black shag with which he constantly filled his pipe. Situations are rarely as desperate as they seem, and as he looked at this one, he persuaded himself that there were qualifying circumstances. While the weather was better, the Matterhorn itself was still covered. Although the Italians had already started, they formed a large party and would therefore be slow moving. Above all, there was talk of 'facilitating the way'. There would be iron staples fixed at places; the stonemason's art or craft would be conscripted to cut a way where no natural steps or holds existed, and all this would take time.

Whymper was not a man to be easily beaten. He was soon downstairs again, airing his tent on the green stretch in front of the inn, checking his equipment, and explaining to Girdlestone that there was still time to reach Zermatt, to try the mountain from the Swiss side, and to reach the summit before the Italians.

All that needed to be settled were the eternal 'ifs'. If he could hire the men needed to take his kit across the Théodule, if he could find an adequate guide in Zermatt, if the weather continued to hold back its help on the Italian side, until he was in position on the Swiss—if all these things fell Whymper's way, he might yet succeed.

It was difficult enough to cope with the first 'if'. Giordano had, as he said in his letter to Sella, 'taken all the competent men away' from Whymper. Girdlestone put it more bluntly, writing later that the Italian had 'bribed one, whom he did not want himself, not to go with Whymper'.

The result was that as the Englishman went the rounds of the huts and chalets he found that one man was ill, that another 'possible' was down the valley in Châtillon, and that even little Luc Meynet the hunchback was too occupied with cheese making to travel over the Théodule to Zermatt.

He returned to the Jomein, still frustrated, still fuming. Lying on the grass, smoking with Girdlestone, cursing Fate, knowing that Giordano was somewhere in the building behind and was keeping tactfully out of sight, Whymper took occasional glances at the Italians whose progress could still be followed through the glass.

The two men had strongly contrasted attitudes to the situation. It was not merely that Girdlestone was still sick, his ambitions pricked by the illness which had exhausted him, while Whymper was in his usual aggressive good health. Girdlestone's Alpine aims were of an altogether milder kind. Mountaineering was merely a part of his European tour; there was much else to be done, much to be seen other than the Alps; and if circumstances kept him down from the summits, well, he would make the best of circumstances and not worry too much.

For Whymper, the whole matter was on a different level. During the previous four seasons he had rarely been rebuffed. Only the Matterhorn had repulsed him again and again, and only the Matterhorn still retained its irresistible fascination. There were, as everyone realised, unclimbed peaks elsewhere in the Alps. But there were none from which men had been thrust back, year after year, despite all efforts.

This, it appeared, was the attraction which the Matterhorn had for Whymper. He emphasised it to Girdlestone, sitting on the grass below the Italian ridge, and although we do not know his words, they stuck in Girdlestone's head so that he later passed on their message to a companion. Whymper was, he said, resolved to climb the Matterhorn. And he was equally resolved, when that was done, to give up mountaineering.

The reason, illuminating in its revelation of how some men then looked at the Alps, seemed simple enough to him. He would give up the pastime simply because there were no more new great mountains to be conquered.

But he still did not know what to do.

It was midday when the first tourist parties could be seen coming down the track from the Théodule. Conditions could not then be so bad in Zermatt, for this was traffic composed of men and women intent on the view, and likely to be put off by bad conditions.

Yet in front of the cavalcade there was a couple who moved at a faster pace. One came with the slow effortless swing of the guide, the other with the confident tread of the hard, fast goer. It seems likely that well before they had reached the inn Whymper had recognised the first figure as young Joseph Taugwalder of Zermatt, son of old Peter who, with T. S. Kennedy, had made that crazy attempt to climb the Matterhorn under winter conditions in January 1862.

The second figure was unknown to him, but he had the cut of an Englishman—a nationality that in much Alpine history has included the Scots, in spite of their continuing and justified protest—and as he arrived Girdlestone and Whymper rose to exchange compliments. The newcomer they learned was Lord Francis Douglas, who now went inside to see Favre while young Joseph disappeared round the back of the inn to make his own enquiries.

A few minutes later Douglas came out again, looking dispirited. He eyed Whymper, the almost legendary young man, only seven years older than himself yet with a string of mountain conquests which he both admired and envied.

Whymper eyed Douglas. He had heard of him. He knew that he had started his mountaineering career two years previously. Great things were prophesied for him, and the way in which he had swung down the path from the Théodule indicated that his pace was at least equal to Whymper's own exacting standards.

So much we can fairly speculate. Yet with Douglas's arrival at the

Jomein there arrives, too, the first unresolved query in the long train of events which were to lead to the conquest of the Matterhorn. Douglas left no record of what was said during his conversation with Whymper; Girdlestone cast no light on it in the letters which he sent back home, while Whymper merely suggests that all initiative came from himself. This is quite possible. He was no man to beat about the bush, it is likely that he came quickly to the point, and the lines of their conversation can fairly be inferred.

"I have been badly let down by the Carrels", Whymper no doubt began. "I wish to leave for Zermatt as soon as possible, but not even a porter is free to help with my things. Could you dispense with young Taugwalder to help me over the Théodule—he could come back immediately if you wanted him?"

Douglas explained that he would be returning to Zermatt himself in about twelve hours' time.

"I imagine that you have one thing in mind, Mr. Whymper"—it was useless for him, either, to beat about any longer. "Old Peter Taugwalder was up above the Hornli a day or so ago and thinks that the Swiss ridge is possible. So do you, I imagine."

Douglas had, he explained, sent up Taugwalder to reconnoitre. The news had been good, but then the bad weather that had delayed Whymper's own attempt from the Italian side had brought matters to a standstill above Zermatt.

"While I was waiting I thought I might as well strengthen my hand", Douglas added. "I came across in the hope, a slight one it seems, of inducing one of the Carrels to come back and help us in an attempt from Zermatt."

Whymper wanted to know whether Almer was still in Zermatt. But Almer had already left. However, that was not enough to deter him. Douglas could see that very little would deter Whymper. He himself, and young Joseph, had come over to Breuil unladen, and there was only one decent thing to do. He would be glad for Taugwalder to give a hand with Whymper's kit.

This first point settled, Whymper went indoors to tell Favre that he wanted his bill. He was no longer marooned at the Jomein and—one can imagine him biting out the words with pleasure—he would be in Zermatt within twenty-four hours.

Favre capitulated. If Whymper was going he might as well go properly. One of his men, he suddenly discovered, would be free after all, and would be glad to help with Mr. Whymper's things. Thus it was arranged. They would leave soon after midnight.

Now, and only now one must imagine, was the next proposal made. They would be in Zermatt on Wednesday the 12th, and most of Douglas's arrangements could be finished before dark, so he would be leaving for the Matterhorn on the Thursday morning.

As for Whymper, guideless, what would he do? The most natural thing in the world, it seemed, would be for him to join Douglas. With his great experience of the mountain, with his skill and his enthusiasm, he would be an accession of strength to any party.

It will forever be impossible to decide who suggested what to whom. But when, in the afternoon of the 11th, it was decided that Douglas and Whymper should attempt the Matterhorn from Zermatt, accompanied by Girdlestone if he had recovered sufficiently, both men must have smiled at the chance which had thus brought them together. Douglas would have a strong ally on a peak that he knew would demand all his ability. Whymper had picked up the services of the one guide who had real knowledge of the Swiss ridge; a guide, moreover, who appeared to have broken through the ring of doubt, ignorance, and almost superstitious awe which had so far kept most Swiss from the upper slopes of the mountain.

Thus it was settled. They would leave at midnight unless the weather took a turn for the worse. 'Happily', as Girdlestone noted, it did so and all were thus able to get a full night's sleep.

CHAPTER SIX

PARTIES MEETING BELOW A MOUNTAIN

THE PARTY OF FIVE LEFT THE JOMEIN for the Théodule Pass and Zermatt at 9am on the morning of Wednesday, July 12th—Whymper, Douglas, Girdlestone, Joseph Taugwalder, and the man whom Favre had agreed should go with them. All except Girdlestone were heavily laden. This is not surprising since they took in one 'carry' not only all Whymper's stores, equipment and ropes, but also the luggage with which Girdlestone was travelling.

The mule path led easily up across green meadows. The weather was still miserable; it was very cold, and they exchanged few words as they plodded on. After three miles, they reached the edge of the easy glacier which sloped more steeply up towards the Col, and here Girdlestone refused to tie down the others to his invalid's pace.

"All right," said his friends, "but we'll wait for you at the top—and we'll have a hot drink ready."

They pushed on and Girdlestone followed, moving now more slowly as the track across the snow steepened and edged nearer to the frontier ridge whose rocky slopes rose on the left.

It was past midday when they all gathered on the crest of the pass at the little hut which did service as an inn. The Théodule, in good weather one of the easiest glacier passes in the Alps, had for long been important—first to the Dukes of Savoy, whose troops had defended a stone redoubt set up here in the 17th century. The soldiers had been followed by the scientists—Saussure who had camped here for three days in a temporary hut, and Forbes who had followed in the early 1840s. A few years later a Valtournanche man had erected a tent, 12 feet long and six or seven feet high, beneath the summit rocks. Here he had habitually stayed with his wife throughout the summer months, offering bread and cheese, wine and the inevitable cognac to all who crossed the pass, and even taking in for the night any traveller hardy enough to share his discomforts for the sake of the sunrise splendour. An Englishman had financed the building of a stone structure in place of the tent and here more than one mountaineer of the Golden Age had come to know the *gardien*, the 'Comte de St. Théodule', a fine old man who had served in Napoleon's Army and who could boast in 1854 that he had two sons serving in the Crimea. By 1865 the stone hut, only six feet to the eaves and some eight feet across, had been augmented by a wooden 'annexe', and to this joint structure Dollfuss-Ausset was already bringing up stocks of fuel and provisions for the men who were to take weather observations for him from the pass throughout the whole of the coming winter.

Here, as promised by his companions, Girdlestone was greeted by hot wine and tea. There was no hurry, and they took their time on this watershed of Europe. In one direction lay Switzerland and the rolling plain that stretched northwards into increasing bleakness; in the other lay the soft south, rich in colour, warm of texture, green and prolific. Looking towards it you could, as a Victorian traveller wrote, 'standing in winter, behold summer beneath you'.

At last they were ready to leave. They trod down the few hundred feet of steep scree that ended at the Théodule Glacier, and here roped up.

The slopes that led down towards Zermatt were easy. But concealed crevasses were common, and they all moved warily, alert for a sudden tug on the rope. They kept to the right of the glacier, making for the outcrop of the Leichenbretter rocks where they picked up the regular mule track from Zermatt. To their left, across the dazzling white slopes of the Upper Théodule Glacier, there rose the Swiss ridge of the Matterhorn, three miles away, seen in profile, and sloping down towards the small peak of the Hornli. Both Whymper and Douglas stopped more than once to gaze across at it, each man working out in his mind what particular problem was likely to be met at this or that point on the rocks.

They were lower than the Hornli when they came to a fork in the track. One branch led due north, straight down to Zermatt, some three miles away; the other went westwards, round the snout of the Théodule Glacier and across the lower extremity of the Furggen Glacier to the chapel which stood by the Schwarzsee.

They took the second branch. The detour was only a short one, and Whymper and Douglas had decided the previous evening to cache the bulk of their supplies beside the Schwarzsee; for the little stone building lay more than 3,000 feet above Zermatt and there was no point in taking more than was necessary down to the village and then carrying it up again the following day.

They made quick work of the two miles separating them from the lake which lies on the rocky plain into which the Swiss ridge spreads out below the Hornli. The building by the lake was a rude affair with narrow slits in the stone walls as windows, an open porch supported on unhewn tree trunks and roofed, as was the chapel itself, with heavy flat stones. Only the roughly-worked cross standing at one end marked it out from the scores of shepherd's huts of the Valais.

Here the laden men off-loaded their packs, and Whymper and Douglas agreed on what should be stacked in a safe place until the following afternoon. There was the tent itself, a 20-pound load. There was the thick and heavy roll of blankets. There were sundry provisions. And there was of course the rope—three different kinds of it. There were, first, two separate 100-foot lengths of Manilla. This was 'Alpine Club' rope, of make and quality which had been approved by the Club after its members had the previous summer tested a number of ropes then in common use. The results of those tests had been unnerving. When the ropes were subjected to the weight of a 12-stone man falling five feet, 'all those plaited ropes which are generally supposed to be so strong, and many most carefully made twisted ropes', commented the Club committee's

The tiny chapel at Schwarzsee

report, 'gave way in such a manner as was very startling to some of our number, who had been in the habit of using these treacherous cords with perfect and most unfounded confidence'. The one which passed all tests was a Manilla and henceforth it was made with a thin thread of red twine running through it, an indication that it would, under all reasonable circumstances, do the job for which it was made.

It was of this rope, certified as one might call it, that Whymper had two 100-foot lengths. However, he also had two other kinds. There was a 150-foot length of even stronger and stouter rope. And there was between 200 and 250 feet of lighter rope which he describes as 'of a kind that I used formerly'. Today it seems almost incredible that it should have been used at all—'sash line' or 'window-cord' would seem fair descriptions. No bigger round than a man's little finger it would, when looked at with the modern eye, appear of the most dubious safety. Whymper himself had apparently used it with confidence, possibly until he had been pulled up by the report of the Club committee. He was now using the 'regulation' Manilla, or even the stouter rope, for the essential business of tying members of a party together. But the thinner line, which he, like others, had used with confidence and ignorance for years, was still carried. However, it was now relegated to other tasks: it was used only for providing fixed ropes, hung from projecting rocks, or for similar jobs where it could be relied upon as a handhold, to steady a man for instance, but where it would never be subjected to the shock of a falling body. However, this was all a finessing of safety measures still only partially understood by many guides, to whom the principles of rope work on a mountain were new if not new-fangled. So far as most of them were concerned a rope was a rope; and so far as this particular coil was concerned it was, in any case, of a kind which Mr. Whymper had himself been using in previous years.

The party stacked their supplies under cover and set off along the path to Zermatt. They were soon making their way down the village street to the Monte Rosa. Here Douglas went up to his room while Whymper paid off Favre's man from the Jomein and made certain that Seiler could accommodate Girdlestone and himself that night.

Then Whymper and Douglas went out to find old Peter Taugwalder. Taugwalder was hardly surprised to see Whymper. He had heard from Christian Almer only a few days previously that the Englishman was at Breuil. He could not imagine Carrel agreeing to cross the frontier and tackle the Swiss ridge, and he must have had more than a suspicion that Whymper would soon be seen in Zermatt. He would as soon climb with Whymper as with any man, and he knew that together with Douglas they would make a strong party. All the same, he would need another guide. Tackling the Matterhorn was still the most daunting enterprise in the Alps and he was taking no chances.

Whymper says merely that he and Douglas 'gave him permission to choose another guide' but it seems likely that there was a slight discussion before everyone agreed on what was necessary. Taugwalder would find a man and come up to the Monte Rosa after dinner when they could decide on the provisions to be taken and make the final arrangements.

1. The Hornli Ridge (centre) from above Zermatt, showing the shoulder above which the party crossed onto the North Face and where the accident occurred

2. The Matterhorn from the Théodule Pass showing the Hornli Ridge in profile
3. Looking up the Hornli Ridge from just above Schwarzsee
4. A view directly up the Hornli Ridge from the start of the climbing

5. *The Italian Ridge and the South Face of the Matterhorn*
6. *The Italian Ridge in profile showing the Col du Lion (centre) and the shoulder*
7. *The Matterhorn from Bruil (Cervinia)*

8. Climbers on the East Face just below the crest of the Hornli Ridge
9. Looking down the Hornli Ridge from about halfway up
10. The upper two-thirds of the Hornli Ridge with the shoulder in the centre of the picture

11. The famous view of the Matterhorn rising above the meadows of Zermatt

One can visualise the two men turning away from Taugwalder's house with a sigh of relief: "Well, that's settled." The weather showed signs of improving. There were formidable difficulties to be overcome by the Italians. Here in Zermatt they could still nourish hopes of being first on the summit. At least there was no other complication. Then, as they came up to the Monte Rosa, they saw, sitting on the guide's wall before them, the figure of Michel Croz.

Tall, bearded, carrying a certain reckless swagger even in the village street, Croz stood up to greet them. It seemed years ago, although in fact it was little more than a fortnight, that Whymper and he had parted in Chamonix, one for his successful first ascent of the Aiguille Verte, the other to hang about for an employer who had engaged him weeks earlier.

Whymper asked where Birkbeck was. Croz explained that so far as he knew Birkbeck was by this time back in England. And, as Douglas went on alone into the Monte Rosa, he explained that he was now engaged by the Rev. Charles Hudson.

Whymper and Croz looked at one another. No record of their conversation exists but Croz would naturally be reluctant to give away his present employer's plans, and equally reluctant to mislead the man with whom he had shared the dangers of so many hazardous places.

But then, in spite of what had happened over in Breuil, Whymper was a difficult man to mislead. He soon sensed the truth. Yes, Croz admitted, they were to try the Matterhorn. He may have added "as soon as possible", but he appears to have given no details.

Perhaps Croz was, after all, not too willing to talk at length to Whymper. His former employer might well have turned to him with at least one awkward question. It was less than three weeks since Croz, together with Almer, had passed over the idea of tackling the east face and had, instead, attempted the dangerous Furggen couloir. Now, with no more knowledge of the mountain, he was prepared to do what he had previously refused to do—to attempt it from the Swiss side, and with a new employer; with an employer whom he had, moreover, come by quite fortuitously. No one will ever know just why he changed his attitude; one can only assume that Hudson's logical exposition of the situation carried more weight than Whymper's.

But if any questions flickered across Whymper's mind he did not ask them. At least, he left no record of the fact. He went indoors and shortly afterwards was seated in the long Wooden *salle-à-manger* with Douglas and Girdlestone. It was early evening, and within the next few hours the fate of the Matterhorn was to be settled—settled by the reactions of four men to the stray chances which had drawn them together. Whymper's account consists of little more than a hundred words. Girdlestone, leaving a lengthy manuscript for posterity, records merely that he sat with them all 'whilst they arranged their plans', and adds that he would 'probably have joined them had not my recovery been so slow'. That is all—although it is not difficult to extrapolate from Whymper's few words, and from the known facts, the story of that evening.

As Whymper, Douglas and Girdlestone ate, they speculated on Hudson's plans. It was possible, of course, that he might first make some other expedition. Croz had been vague, and both Whymper and Douglas warmed themselves with hopes that they alone would be out on the mountain tomorrow.

Then, just as they were finishing their meal, Hudson and Hadow strode in. Both had, during the last few hours, achieved a certain notoriety among their fellow guests as the rash mortals who were planning to scale that terrifying rock pyramid which reared up at the end of the valley.

"Been looking at your Matterhorn again, sir?" someone called across to Hudson.

They had, in fact, been making a final reconnaissance. "Yes, it's all settled now", Hudson replied. "We'll be off soon after five tomorrow."

Whymper and Douglas exchanged glances. A moment later they went down the stairs, followed by Girdlestone. Below, Whymper turned to Douglas. "How many will that make us?" he asked. "There's you and

I"—and here Girdlestone confirmed what they knew already: that he wasn't up to that sort of work as yet.

"Anyway," Douglas added, "there'll be four of us, counting Taugwalder and whoever he brings with him. There will be Hudson and his friend and Croz, which makes at least seven of us all on the same ridge."

Whymper thought that Croz might be taking another man as porter, which would mean eight men in all.

Today, when the more popular ridges of the Alps are festooned with mountaineers, it is difficult to realise the dismay which such an idea aroused in the climbers of the Golden Age. Yet even today the Swiss ridge of the Matterhorn is notorious for the ease with which loose rocks can be dislodged, for the dangers of the cannonade which can be thoughtlessly started by one party and can bring disaster to another a few hundred feet down the mountain. A century ago the problem was immeasurably larger. Wind and weather, it is true, continue with their process of fracturing the rocks, of levering them loose, of giving the lie to that phrase 'the everlasting hills'. Yet the passage of countless parties acts as a constant scavenger, cleaning the ridges of at least some of the rocky debris. In 1865 the mountains were, by comparison, unswept—littered with loose material which it was difficult not to dislodge and which provided a constant danger.

It was, as Whymper put it, 'undesirable that two independent parties should be on the mountain at the same time with the same object'.

He and Douglas waited until the other two Englishmen had finished their meal, and then went up to them. Whymper had a very slight acquaintance with Hudson. Each well knew the other's reputation.

"We, also, are setting out for the Matterhorn tomorrow morning", Whymper said. "Might I suggest that you join us, sir?"

Hadow had stood back, but as Hudson admitted that this would indeed be a good idea, it was clear that the younger man was included in his acceptance. Here a minor, temporary, but almost certainly perceptible doubt made itself felt.

Whymper knew that Hudson's ability was at least equal to his own. He knew nothing of Hadow's. He had, it is true, been willing to consider taking Walter Hargreaves, Girdlestone's untried companion, across the Col de Tâlèfre some ten days previously. But the Matterhorn was another matter. He had no wish to take a passenger on this particular expedition, and he was not willing to let undue politeness saddle him with one. He says that before 'admitting' Hadow to the proposed combined party, he 'took the precaution to inquire what he had done in the Alps'. One can imagine him enquiring without undue ceremony.

Hudson's reply, one of two solitary sentences that Whymper quotes from the whole of that evening's discussion was, as well as he later remembered: "Mr. Hadow has done Mont Blanc in less time than most men."

This was of course the exploit of a few days previously. It showed energy, enthusiasm, athleticism. It did not necessarily reveal any particular mountain prowess of the kind that would be needed on the Matterhorn, and it appears that Whymper was hardly impressed.

Hudson, according to Whymper, went on to mention 'several other excursions that were unknown' to him—possibly hard walks of the 60-mile-a-day variety which Hudson enjoyed, since the 19 year-old destined for the Matterhorn had made only one previous mountain ascent before that of Mont Blanc.

Whymper turned to Hudson with a further question, and there is little doubt as to what it was: "Yes—but is he really experienced enough for this sort of work?" Hudson's reply, quoted by Whymper more than once, without qualification, almost as if in justification, was a simple: "I consider he is a sufficiently good man to go with us."

Whymper must have known that he was taking a chance. So must Hudson. Douglas, in all probability, was just as much aware of the fact. But they pushed the risk into the back of their minds. After all, events were now relentlessly driving towards a moment when the Matterhorn would be climbed. In the face of that fact reason was tipped overboard, and in their own sober way each man no doubt felt like Yeats's airman for whom 'the years to come seemed waste of breath'. They, too, drove willingly to their own tumult in the clouds.

Thus was the matter arranged, not too hastily had the ascent been that of a well known and not too difficult mountain, but with what appears to have been astonishing casualness in view of the Matterhorn's reputation. A slightly quicker recovery would have meant Girdlestone's addition to the party. M'Cormick, arriving to join Hudson after he had left for the Matterhorn, was invited to follow on and catch them up. Robertson, now making his way to Zermatt by the High Level Route, had been casually invited a few days earlier; Birkbeck and Kennedy had been excluded only by illness and the timetable of a honeymoon respectively.

At first glance the haphazardness of the planning, if planning it can be called, would seem to be of the sort that brings down the admonition of coroners. So does the curious arrangement by which it was agreed that no one person should be leader. 'We deliberated together whenever there was occasion', wrote Whymper, who added that he would have been content to place himself under Hudson's orders. There was to be joint leadership, which in some cases means no leadership at all.

Yet all this is the verdict of hindsight and the slow careful sifting of facts throughout the years. Today, well over a century later, it is easy enough to argue that the expedition should have been arranged more tightly, that one person should have been in undisputed command. In a logical, meticulously thought out world this would have been so. Yet Henry might as well have encouraged his men into the breach with careful injunctions about the order of their going. There are times when wars cannot be won that way, nor mountains climbed. This appeared to be one of them.

One remaining question was that of the guides. Earlier on, Taugwalder had insisted on a second man for Douglas and Whymper. But that would swell the total of the party to seven—a large number of men to be moving together on the mountain. Hudson considered that Croz and old Peter Taugwalder would be sufficient, and no one raised any objection. But they would put it to the guides themselves. Croz was ready at hand, while Taugwalder would be coming up any minute to complete arrangements, see Seiler to ensure that the right provisions were ready, and to agree on the hour at which they should start.

It was a simple enough matter. Croz was happy, and Taugwalder agreed, although he had one reservation. He was optimistic, but they might yet find the going as difficult as the earlier pessimists had forecast. At first—as young Peter remembered the story years later—his father's proposal was 'to get two other guides and make up two parties'. This may have been a suggestion that the single party should, in fact, climb on two ropes. Hudson disagreed, but it is not necessary to believe young Peter's claim that he 'modestly thought he and his companions were all better than guides'. All that he probably did was reiterate his belief that the four Englishmen made up a party strong enough to need only two guides.

Eventually, a compromise was agreed upon. Taugwalder would bring two of his sons with him. They would merely act as porters and help carry the provisions up to a high bivouac on the mountain before returning to Zermatt. One thing would of course help. Whymper already had some 600 feet of rope safely cached up at the Schwarzsee, so that there would be no need to take anyone else's. Even Hudson's steel cable could be left behind. All was finally agreed, and it was arranged that they would rendezvous at 5 o'clock the following morning.

There was no argument. All was settled amicably. Then someone looked at his watch. "We'll have to be up early", he warned. They said goodnight to Taugwalder who made off down the village street. Then they went upstairs to bed as the other visitors took a last glass of wine or strolled about in the yard, tasting the twilight, breathing in the thick country smell and listening to the persistent tumble and rush of the Visp which alone broke the silence.

PART THREE
THE TRAGEDY

Chapter seven

Ascent

Thursday, July 13th, 1865, dawned clear and bright, with the promise of a diamond-sharp day. Having lowered the clouds for the necessary periods throughout the last week, whatever Gods may be now raised them without reserve, quickly dispersing even the early morning mists so that the Pennine Alps were soon revealed in their full glory, clean-cut, free of fresh snow, a mountain landscape so detailed that the third dimension appeared to have been withdrawn from it. As the party of Englishmen came down to the deserted dining room of the Monte Rosa soon after 4am it seemed that you could almost stretch out and touch the most distant peaks. It was a morning to make the blood run faster, dispel doubt, quicken the sense of great things at hand.

As they sat over coffee, Hudson remembered M'Cormick. From the known facts, it is not difficult to reconstruct the ensuing conversation "Seiler will see that he doesn't come up unless he has everything that's necessary. Anyway, it's only courtesy to leave him a note."

He called for a sheet of paper, took out his silver pencil, and began writing. 'My Dear M'C,' he started, 'We and Whymper are just off to try the Cervin. You can hear about our movements from the landlord of the Monte Rosa Hotel. Follow us, if you like. We expect to sleep out tonight, and to make the attempt tomorrow. Please give an eye to Campbell as long as you are with him, and take him to the Riffel, in case you go there. We expect to be back tomorrow. It is possible we might be out a second night, but not likely—Ever yours affectionately, C. Hudson.' He turned to Seiler, hovering courteously within call on such an occasion as this. "Mr. M'Cormick should have arrived yesterday", he said. "See that he gets this as soon as he comes in."

In searching for his pencil he had half emptied his pockets and he now turned to Seiler again. "You may as well take this", he said. "We shan't need it on the mountain." He handed him two 20-franc Napoleons, some lesser French money, and a ten-pound English banknote—then added his silver pencil.

Seiler meticulously started to list the money, and as he did so Douglas handed across his wallet and a handful of small change. The others did the same, while young Hadow in addition took off two gold rings, put a silver watch and gold watch chain in his purse and handed this also to Seiler.

"Perhaps you would ask Croz if he has anything he wants to leave with you", said Hudson, and Seiler went out to where Croz was already conferring with the Taugwalders. Conferring, that is, as far as was possible. For while Croz spoke French, he had only a smattering of German. Old Peter Taugwalder understood little more than German and the local patois. Young Peter, however, had done his military service in the French speaking canton of Vaud, and the French he had picked up in the Army enabled him to carry on at least a rough-and-ready conversation with Croz. In addition, he knew the odd word or so of English. This helped. It may even have been sufficient when the business in hand was the dividing out of loads and the simple matters in which sign language can replace words. When the problem was the abstract one of responsibility, the balancing of one set of chances against another, the implementation of detail, the lack of more effective communication was to prove fatal.

Outside the guides' room at the back of the Monte Rosa, Hudson and Whymper checked the loads. The provisions seemed ample enough. No record remains of what they were but one can assume the customary legs of mutton, the loaves, the strong butter, above all the wine bags which Whymper himself was to carry. Hudson, Hadow, and the guides all had their own blankets. The loads would of course have been bigger still had not Whymper and Douglas cached much equipment up at the Schwarzsee chapel the previous afternoon.

Even so, all the men were well laden as they said goodbye to Seiler. It

was just 5.30am and they walked in couples, as Whymper put it, 'to ensure steady motion', a guide by the side of each Englishman. Zermatt
was used to such sights, even though this one had a special quality. It was
not every day that two men of the calibre of Hudson and Whymper
formed part of one party. It was not every day that men went out seriously, and apparently with high hopes of success, on an effort to climb
the Matterhorn. It was a great occasion. But among the older folk there
was some shaking of heads.

There were no doubts, no uncertainties, among the British party. They
were all uncomplicated men, like most true mountaineers; what is more,
in the 1860s there was no need to pretend that they were anything else.
The excuse of scientific enquiry was no longer really necessary; all that
needed to be said, at least among themselves, was that they were about to
enjoy an expedition. Yet each had his own reason: for Hudson, mountaineering combined a release of animal energy with a delicate probing
into what his friend, the Reverend Hereford George, called 'the arcana
of Nature'. For Hadow, the exploit would lift him into the ranks of men.
For Whymper there was still that last unclimbed peak which continued
to defy him. As for Douglas—Douglas regarded the enterprise as a test-
ing, dangerous adventure, worth doing for its own sake; he climbed, so
far as one can gather, just for the hell of it. In an age when most mountaineers conformed to a type, the amateurs were thus of intriguingly diverse natures—Hudson wrapped in a kindly woolliness; Hadow eager;
Whymper near arrogant; and Douglas with a mind already being trained
to accept the hazards of command. All were to run true to form.

They were dressed as much for the English countryside as for the
high Alps. The age of neatly cut climbing breeches and puttees had not
yet arrived, and their clothes were of the loosely fitting, old and vari-
egated kind. Whymper was distinguished by his white slop trousers and
his wide brimmed felt hat, a double of which was also worn by Croz, a
present brought from London by Whymper as a reminder of previous
campaigns together. Croz now also wore the loose fitting, jacket length
blue smock which he had purchased in Martigny a day or so previously,

but the rest were clad only in the drably miscellaneous garments which would have seemed fitting for potterers in a quiet English garden.

The lack of properly designed mountaineering clothes was emphasised by the flapping trouser ends which only on occasions were contained by improvised fabric 'gaiters' tied with string or by canvas contraptions which were a cross between anklet and spat. It was emphasised, also, by their boots. These were stout, but were in no respect specially built for mountain work. Most were merely hobbed, although Hudson's may well have been equipped with the double-headed nails, not unlike the later Tricouni, which could be bought at the Pavillon on the Montenvert, and which screwed into the sole of the boot. However, this suggestion that certain of their equipment might bear a resemblance to that of today was not supported by the footwear of the younger men. Lord Francis Douglas wore not boots but merely shoes, hobbed, it is true, but giving no support to the ankle on difficult rocks. Hadow wore boots but the hobs were approaching uselessness and danger, having been worn down and polished by continual contact with pathway and track. The iron tipping round the heels, which a man would use in descending steep rock, was in the same smooth and slippery state.

No one gave a thought to such things as the party passed through the village, followed the left bank of the Visp up to the second bridge across the stream from the Zmutt Glacier, and then struck up the steeper track towards the Schwarzsee. There was no need to think about much at all, for the plans which they had made the previous evening had ruled out any attempt to reach the summit that day. Whymper, obsessed as he still was by fear that the Italians might forestall them, yet knew the dangers of a too quick one-day dash. Instead, they would camp out at some convenient place above the Hornli, leaving only a few thousand feet for the following day. That last few thousand feet had until now been dismissed as impracticable by almost all mountaineers, but only a handful had seen it at close quarters and none had inspected it carefully.

The whole day was therefore before them, and they took their time— at least, they took their time judged by the standards of such men as

Hudson and Whymper. In fact, heavily laden though they were, they had covered three miles from Zermatt, ascended the three thousand feet to the Schwarzsee, within two hours of leaving the Monte Rosa. It was just 7.30am when they reached the little chapel, off-loaded their packs, and started to congratulate themselves that the weather was really going to be as good as the guides had forecast first thing.

They spent nearly an hour lolling in the sun, eating the traditional second breakfast, and portioning out Whymper's tent, ropes, and provisions between the Taugwalders and Croz.

Then, at 8.20am, they set off again. Their route lay round the sharp peak of the Hornli, along the rough ground which stretches between the ridge of the peak on the right and the moraine of the Furgg Glacier which reaches out from the left. They gained height gradually, inclining to the right all the time and thus making an upward traverse so that by 9.30am they had reached the ridge itself. Here, once again, they halted and faced the mountain.

Behind lay the Hornli, now curiously insignificant, almost unrecognisable as the shapely summit seen from Zermatt, and throwing down the easy ridge on which the party stood. They were at the lowest point on this ridge. Before them it rose brusquely with what appeared to be increasing steepness; narrowing, sharpening but leading upwards and ever upwards towards the summit of the Matterhorn some 6,000 feet above them. From this ridge, which led almost centrally up the bulk of the mountain as they saw it, there sloped down the east face on the left, the north face on the right, one dropping to the Furgg Glacier, the other to the Zmutt. These faces were now seen, as was the ridge itself, virtually end on. The foreshortening of the perspective which can give such an illusory impression was here at its strongest, and it was difficult not to believe that the word 'vertical' could almost be applied to the cataract of slabs and gullies and pinnacles and multitudinous rock-features which made up this side of the Matterhorn.

They would not get a better viewpoint. Here they halted, and both guides and amateurs studied the detailed features of the mountain through their glasses. The east face and the ridge which bounded it would at first present the obviously less difficult options, although higher up, where the summit appeared to lean over like a wave breaking towards the east, it was the northern slope which was less steep. Each man had his own view, his own preference; yet certainly Hudson and Whymper, certainly Croz and old Peter Taugwalder, knew that the only way of discovering exactly what the difficulties really were was 'to rub one's nose on the mountain'.

They set off again at 10.25am, still unroped since the going remained easy. They kept to the crest of the ridge wherever possible, moving to left or right only where a minor rock tower, an awkward slab, or some similar feature momentarily barred the way. Either Hudson or Whymper went first, chipping an occasional step with their ice axes where a patch of snow or ice had to be crossed. Even though the mountain was in good condition, these patches were frequent. For they were now more than 9,000 feet up and it was not only the great panorama, opening up behind them as the minutes passed, but also the crispness of the air, which left them in no doubt as to the height they had already gained.

Earlier in the morning Whymper had been perpetually stopping to look through the glass towards the summit, always fearful that what experience told him were mere rocks might in fact be figures. Now, closer up under the flank of the mountain, he was deprived of that preoccupying worry since the summit was out of sight, hidden by the rocks immediately above.

They climbed on thus for nearly an hour, going easily, chatting occasionally, until they distinguished up above them on the ridge ahead a pyramidical pile of stones nearly six feet high. The leading men stopped at it and as Taugwalder came up he patted it affectionately and told them that it was Kennedy's cairn. Then, as well as he could, he explained how he and Peter Perrin had come up from Zermatt on that January day more than three years ago, with T. S. Kennedy. They had climbed a few hundred feet beyond where they all now stood, but the conditions—and old Peter shook his head as though he thought that Mr. Kennedy must have been even madder than most who came to such places where you could neither grow things nor keep sheep, and which were avoided even by self respecting chamois. Trying the Matterhorn in January indeed! He raised his eyes to Heaven.

The party was now on the outer fringe of known territory. Five years previously, the three Parker brothers had come as far as this without guides and had then continued to climb upwards, partly on the east face, partly on the ridge itself, until bad weather and lack of time forced them to turn back. Whymper himself had dug out from Samuel Parker as much information as he could. He appears to have got little—not through any lack of cooperation on Parker's part but because neither Parker nor his brothers had studied the mountain carefully. Their effort had been more of an isolated *tour de force* than the opening shot in a campaign, and they had brought back a bare record rather than detailed information. For all practical purposes the mountain was unknown above the spot where the party now stood.

It was shortly after 11.30am that the Matterhorn sprung its first surprise. Hudson, Whymper and the guides all agreed that they should leave the ridge for the eastern face which from their viewpoint on the ridge, appeared, less precipitous than had been expected. Once again, either Whymper or Hudson went first. They moved out on to broadish slabs, up which they trod with relative ease. Here and there a hand was needed, but nothing more. They went on, and higher. They continued to gain height with no difficulty at all. Surprise turned to incredulity for, as Whymper later put it, places which had looked entirely impracticable from below were found 'so easy that we could run about'.

All at once, the mountain instinct which had forced Taugwalder to reconnoitre the Swiss ridge, and the belief which had begun to grow in Whymper's mind both became justified. Much of the huge east face, seen almost flat-on from Zermatt, was nothing more than a deception. It rose not vertically, but at an angle easing back from the vertical, not at 90 degrees but at 60 degrees or less. The latter, for those with no head for heights, can appear steep out of all proportion—as those who have ascended the pyramids will know—but for the mountaineer the problems which it presents are of a totally different order.

This was soon demonstrated to the party on the Matterhorn on the morning of July 13th, 1865. It was not literally true that they could 'go anywhere' on the east face. But they were all able to move without trouble, turning minor difficulties by easier alternatives.

By midday they had reached a height of about 11,000 feet, less than 4,000 feet below the summit. Here, on a flat patch of rocks, protected by a short near vertical wall from any boulders that might fall, they decided to pitch their tents.

It may at first be wondered why they did not press on higher. Some eight or nine hours of daylight remained. They were well provisioned. There was, above all for Whymper if not for the others, a personal anguish about the possibility of Carrel and the Italians reaching the summit first. It is easy to speculate on such matters now that men—with muscles, one must imagine, no better than those of Hudson, Whymper and the guides—have climbed the mountain in well under a day, out from Zermatt and back to it. Even at the turn of the century between four and five hours was reckoned sufficient for the climb to the summit from the hut erected a few hundred feet below the campsite of the 1865 party.

All this is to disregard that the Matterhorn of today is not the Matterhorn of the Golden Age. Physically, its difficulties have been minimised by the fixing of ropes, the extent of its loose rock reduced by the 'gardening' of innumerable parties. Psychologically, the change is even greater. Neither old Peter nor Croz really expected to find the infuriate demons of legend on the summit; but one has a shrewd suspicion that they kept fingers crossed until they had confirmed the fact with their own eyes.

There was, moreover, the size of the party. Had merely Whymper, Douglas and old Peter ascended across the east face, it is possible that they would have pressed on upwards, hoping that by moving fast they would get to the top and return far enough to trick themselves out in a possible bivouac before darkness fell. Hudson, Hadow and Croz might well have tried the same. But after the two Taugwalder sons had been sent back the present party would still number six; they would move more slowly than a smaller party even on easy ground, and if any real difficulties arose, they would move far more slowly. They did not yet know what those difficulties might be. There might well be no comparable campsite higher up.

They decided that this was the place, swung the leather straps of the packs from their shoulders, and began to unload. First they had a bite of bread and a slice of meat, a lump of cheese, and a swig from the goatskin winebags that Whymper had been carrying since they left Zermatt. He still retained his earlier suspicions of guides as 'large consumers of meat and drink', and when there had been a stop for refreshment lower down that morning, he had surreptitiously topped up the bags with water, the results being, as he puts it, 'considered a good omen, and little short of miraculous'.

It was now decided that Croz and young Peter should reconnoitre the route for the following day while the others prepared the camp site. The two men shared a common language, even though young Peter's share was a small one. They were soon off, cutting up and across the snow gullies which scored the east face and dropped to the Furgg Glacier. Within minutes they were out of sight, hidden by a rib of rock which concealed much of the upper part of the east face, although for a while their voices came down through the clear air, intermingling with the receding chink of their axes against the rock.

The rest of the party set about levelling the site, moving stones and slabs to form a rough wall on the outer side of the rocky shelf, and then watching as Whymper proudly assembled his tent—one of the first, as he no doubt explained, to be designed especially for mountain work. They finished the layout of the campsite. They stacked the provisions, saw that the ropes were laid out carefully where they would not get trodden on, brewed up tea, and basked in the sun. The weather still showed no signs of changing. Even old Peter, as pessimistic as most guides, could see no hint of it.

For Whymper, the blue skies, warm sun, freedom from mist, all cut both ways. It was now, he totted up, some 60 hours since Carrel and his party had left the Jomein. He knew that the way had to be 'prepared'. He knew that as late as yesterday morning—only yesterday morning—when Douglas and he had left for the Théodule, things were not really moving, for Giordano was then still at Favre's. All the same, he continued to worry.

From time to time there came down to the tent platform the distant clatter of stones loosened by Croz and young Peter higher on the mountain. It seemed to be coming from a long way up.

Then, after they had been away for nearly three hours, the two men could be seen returning down across the east face. There seemed to be much excitement. They were shouting, and old Peter was asked what the indistinguishable flurry of patois meant.

One can imagine the dismay on Taugwalder's face as he turned to an anxious Whymper and Hudson with the words: "Gentlemen, they say it is no good."

But Taugwalder was wrong. As young Peter and Michel Croz got nearer, it was possible to distinguish properly what they were saying. Whymper quotes the excited words although he does not say who used them—probably Croz: "Nothing but what was good; not a difficulty, not a single difficulty! We could have gone to the summit and returned today easily!"

This was quite possibly true. But it was an age in which the *coup de gráce* was given by the amateur, and peaks were kept for employers. Croz and young Peter had dutifully returned without going on to the top; but, as Hudson and Whymper no doubt reminded them, they had not been able to check, on the ground, finger and foot to rock, what the remaining difficulties really were.

Yet the news was immensely better than any of them had dared hope—the only nagging annoyance being, certainly for Whymper and possibly for Hudson, that this key to the Matterhorn, staring them in the face for so long, had for so long been overlooked. However, they would remedy that tomorrow.

There was still six hours or so before dark. Whymper took out his pocket sketchbook, a small oblong only a few inches either way and, propped up against the rocks, began drawing the mountain outlines. Hudson and Hadow traversed across the slope, collecting geological specimens. Douglas just basked in the sun, discussing with old Peter their joint exploits of a week ago and asking what would be worth doing the following season.

As the shadows lengthened, conversation began to die down. There was hardly a cloud in the sky. It was so still that you could almost hear the world turning. First one stretch of the distant valleys, then another, grew grey and dusky, and then indistinct as the light left them and their inhabitants began the evening life of those who live between high mountain walls. Up above, the snowfields were aglow, and the eight men gathered at the tent platform, silently watching the slowly changing pageant that is one reward of those who camp in high places.

The chill began to strike as the sun went down. Hudson brewed up tea. Whymper made coffee, while the guides relished the thick soup which was heated amid the acrid smoke from the fuel they had carried. More than once they must have wondered what the Italians were doing, where they were, how high they were, and what success they had so far achieved.

Had they but known it, the Italians were separated from them by only some 1,200 yards of mountain. But they were camping that night at 13,000 feet, some 2,000 feet higher than the British party and only 1,800 feet below the summit.

The stars gently took over from the dying sun, and the men retired to their blanket bags. Whymper, Douglas and the three Taugwalders squeezed themselves into the tent of which Whymper was so justifiably proud. Hudson, Hadow and Croz remained outside.

At first they gossiped. Then old Taugwalder struck up one of the Valais songs. Croz replied as a true Savoyard with one of his own. The friendly rivalry between two fine professionals, each with his own idiosyncrasies, each with his strong beliefs and prejudices built up over the years, flickered between the two groups. Both men looked back to that time, only a decade ago, when the very idea of attempting the Matterhorn would have been derided—not only in Zermatt and Chamonix, but everywhere in the Alps, by professionals and amateurs alike. And now Mr. Whymper and Mr. Hudson appeared to have the matter in their own hands at last. What a change there had been in ten short years! It was impossible to know what men would try next.

The crossfire of comment died down. Then they slept. 'I dreamed all night long that I was standing on the top of the Matterhorn and had sent a jodel down into the valley loud enough to be heard in Zermatt', young Peter remembered. 'Then, suddenly, I was alone on the summit. I could not see the others anywhere and the terror of it woke me up. It was about 2.00am and the others were also beginning to stir.'

Outside the tent, Hudson was already preparing tea. The rest wriggled from their blanket bags, still only half awake, still wrapped in that awful atmosphere of regret and disbelief that is apt to envelope mountaineers at 2.00am on even the most exciting of expeditions.

The starlight enabled them to move about outside, and as they gulped down the steaming tea the guides began muttering over the loads, talking over what should be taken, separating the food, repacking and then deciding that if the arrangement was not ideal it would just have to do.

As the sky began to lighten and they made their final preparations, checking that their laces were tight, feeling each pocket to make sure that pipe or spyglass or matchbox was in its customary place, old Peter came across to Whymper and Hudson. With the six of them—Whymper and Hudson, Douglas and Hadow, and two guides—it would be difficult to portion out the loads conveniently. Young Peter had done a good job in reconnoitring the slopes above with Croz. He was young but he was already experienced. He had been up the Breithorn, the Weisshorn, he had.... Both Whymper and Hudson must have known what was coming.

Yes, they agreed. Young Peter could come on with them instead of going back to Zermatt with his brother. There was the tent to take back, it was true, and the blanket bags, but it would do Joseph no harm to have a difficult load. So that was settled.

As they got ready to leave, Whymper noticed the men taking one of the tent poles and tying it on to a pack. The explanation came quickly enough. This would be a great victory. Victory demanded a flag and a flag on the Matterhorn demanded a flag pole. It was as simple as that.

Yet it was not only the Valaisians who were superstitious. The English, in their own fashion, had to be careful of their gods. Whymper expostulated that it was tempting Providence. His expostulations were for once disregarded. The tent pole would be taken to the top.

At last all was ready. It was now past 3.00am and a long bar, pure gold in colour, began to appear along the eastern horizon. The youngest Taugwalder wished them well. Old Peter gave him a few final crisp words of instruction, and the party prepared to move off and up across the slopes which had been reconnoitred the previous day.

It is difficult not to believe that before they did so Hudson suggested that they should pray. Below Mont Blanc, often ascended, calling mainly for stamina and good luck, Hudson had gone to M'Cormick's room and there had prayed for success. Here, on the most formidable unclimbed peak of the Central Alps, in circumstances more impressive, more dangerous and more moving, with the stars growing fainter and the light swelling up from the east, Hudson surely wished to ask for God's help in the enterprise ahead. The others, if not enthusiastic, would feel that no harm would be done.

It was just 3.30am on July 14th as Hudson, Whymper, Douglas and Hadow, Croz and the two Taugwalders, assembled by the vagaries of fortune, set out for the last 3,800 feet of the Matterhorn.

Now that mountaineering has moved on apace, and the assault of even a minor peak can attract the logistics of a military venture, the attempt wears a casual and slightly haphazard air. Yet in this respect the Matterhorn party was typical of many others, though its purpose was sharpened by the uncomplicated sporting hope that they would reach the summit before the Italians. Even so it would be wrong to lay on to it too heavily the overtones of dire personal and national interest that can be a feature of modern mountaineering. It would be fine to get to the summit before anyone else; it would be doubly fine to beat the Italians. There was no doubt about these feelings. But one cannot help believing that they differed in one way from their counterparts a century later. No one had yet begun seriously to believe that mountaineering, was, would be, or ever should be, anything like a business. When the holiday jaunt was over, the amateurs would go back to England and continue with the world's real work. The guides would return to the proper business of subsistence farming, of cheese making, of cow keeping and goat keeping that they rightly appreciated formed the economic bread and butter of their existence. Only for Whymper were things a little different.

The light heartedness of the party which now scrambled up towards the rib obscuring the eastern slope of the mountain from the tent platform was natural enough. Two things combined to make it exceptional— its size, and the fact that no one was quite certain who was actually in command. It appears to have been tacitly assumed that the six men— now augmented to seven by the addition of young Peter—would climb on a single rope when the difficulties of the ground made roping necessary. All would be physically tied by a length or by a series of lengths. Now the principles of rope work are complex and not briefly to be explained. But it can be said that while two men who are tied together can be mutually supporting, and while this mutual support may be increased by a third, there comes a point when the balance of numbers swings to disadvantage; and when the addition of further members to a 'rope', as the group is collectively known, is apt to increase rather than to decrease the chances of disaster. Such was to be the case on the Matterhorn.

More important was the question of leadership, that intangible holding of the reins in difficult places, that quality of command resting beneath the surface yet ever ready to appear as events move towards crisis. Leadership on the Matterhorn was, according to one's viewpoint, either nonexistent or of the troika variety. Croz, the most experienced of the guides, might have held it as by custom—another guide had once said: "Herr you are master in the valley: I am master here." Yet on the Matterhorn it was not quite so simple. Both Hudson, 'almost as good as a guide', and Whymper with his intuitive feel for what could be done on a mountain, were very different from the normal run of amateurs. The difficulty arose from that very fact. It might have been possible for Croz to control the party jointly with his employer, Hudson; it might have been possible for him to do so with Whymper, his former employer. As it was, the matter went by default and in the growing light the party turned to the mountain with amiable high spirits but with no one man definitely bearing the hazards of command.

One by one, they breasted the rib of rock. One by one they viewed the scene with amazement. Before them rose the east face, a massive series of giant steps, leading upwards for 3,000 feet until, some 700 feet below the summit, the angle altered. To Whymper, it was 'a huge natural staircase'. That description was a mountaineer's, and to other men the sight would have been formidable enough. Yet the prospect was startlingly different from what had been expected. The position of such grandstands as the Riffelberg and the Gornergrat, had led men to view the east face even more 'flat on' than when it was seen from Zermatt; to look at it so that the manner in which the individual steps receded, much like the successive steps of the pyramids, was concealed by perspective. One had appeared to be looking, not at the side of a pyramid but at the side of a skyscraper. Now this was seen to be largely an illusion; only for the last few hundred feet, where the rocks steepened and from some angles gave the appearance of bending over into space, did there appear to be any difficulties likely to hamper such a party as now faced the mountain.

It is not clear, either from Whymper's account or from that of young Peter Taugwalder, exactly who now took the lead; or, in fact, whether any of the party as yet put on the rope. For all except Hadow the going was easy and it seems likely that up much of the face each man picked his own route. Obstructions, Whymper says, 'could always be turned to the right or to the left'. Young Peter, speaking of 'Douglas' but very probably referring to Douglas Hadow, says that he 'had great difficulty in putting his feet down in the steps, and several times he slipped. However, I held his legs firm in the steps with my hands almost all the time.'

The central section of the Hornli seen in profile and described by Whymper as 'a huge natural staircase'

They scrambled up, higher and higher, moving almost anywhere at will, not feeling the need for belays, giving one another an occasional hand at places, keeping an eye on Hadow.

It was light, without a shred of mist, and as they climbed upwards the clear morning brilliance of the early sun moved down the mountain to meet them. Soon they were standing in its warming rays, confident now as they had never been before.

They had bivouacked high enough, got off to a good start, and were moving easily. Gnawing away at Whymper there was still the fear that the Italians might be even nearer the summit on the far side of the mountain. Yet he felt almost unjustifiably sure of himself. There was some scent of success in the air and they hardly bothered to hurry.

In spite of the easy going, they took about three hours to rise 1,800 feet, taking it comfortably, husbanding themselves for the more difficult work that might yet appear.

At 6.20am they decided to halt. The guides took off their loads, and for half an hour they enjoyed a second breakfast, facing the bright sun and looking out across the dazzling whiteness of the Furgg Glacier far below. It was here perhaps that they first began to appreciate the great height that they had already reached. The Théodule, away in the distance, was far beneath them. They were higher than the Klein Matterhorn, the peak which rose beyond the pass, and only a few hundred feet below the summit of the Breithorn. Behind them rose the steepening east face, before them lay but space.

To Hadow in particular there may well have come, for the first time, a sense of the deepening gulf below. It is true that this great east face sloped not at the average of 70 degrees which had been anticipated, but at little more than half that. Yet perspective is a curious thing which has its own revenge on the human perception. The slope which rises at a mere 45 degrees looks vertical when seen face on and a mere bagatelle when seen in profile. But the inexperienced traveller finds when standing upon it that it has regained all its original verticality while he was looking elsewhere. Thus to Hadow there may well have come a sudden realisation that they had now entered a kingdom where mistakes were not readily overlooked.

At 6.50am they loaded up and moved off. There was a constant, though small, danger from stones dislodged by the growing heat of the sun from the upper slopes, and they kept well to their right, near the ridge on to which they could hope to retreat if there came a sudden warning clatter from above. Twice they followed the ridge itself but found it more difficult than the face, and on each occasion bore out to the left once again.

They had been on the move for another three hours when, at 9.55am, they stopped once again, and joined one another. During the first spell of nearly three hours they had been climbing at about 540 feet an hour, a rate which was certainly not limited by the ground and was probably accounted for by a combination of Hadow's inexperience and the size of the party. Even though unroped, the need to keep relatively close together—thus minimising dangers from loose stones—would tend to slow the pace. During the second period they had been rising at only 390 feet an hour, an indication that even though the ground was immensely easier than had been expected it had by this time to be treated with respect.

Now, a few minutes before 10.00am, they were at 14,000 feet. They were higher than any men had yet been on the Matterhorn—at least, so they hoped. Less than 800 feet of the mountain still rose above them. But, as they could see, the east face now steepened into a perpendicular wall up which they could not hope to move. They would have to take to the ridge, or to move across it on to the north face. Or—a thought that does not appear to have entered their heads—they would have to admit that there was, after all, no practicable route up the Swiss ridge.

There is only one indication that the party now realised they had reached the watershed of their expedition. This is Whymper's statement that they halted here for a whole 50 minutes. Fifty minutes! Almost an hour while, for all they knew, the Italians might be scrambling up the last few feet on to the summit ridge that had become the aim of all human hope and desire!

Young Peter Taugwalder merely records that they left their rucksacks and provisions here but it seems likely that there was some humming and hawing before they finally, at 10.55am crossed the ridge on to the north face.

Before this, they roped up. Whymper, writing in the *Journal de Zermatt* 30 years later, says that they now did so for the first time. Taugwalder, reminiscing more than half a century later, says that they had been roped from the start—one of those occasions on which the balance of likelihood goes to Whymper.

It was Croz who had taken the decision to move on to the north face and it was Croz who now led across the ridge and on to the uppermost 700 sloping feet of the mountain. Behind him came Whymper, Hudson, Hadow, old Peter, then Lord Francis Douglas and young Peter bringing up the rear.

Years later Whymper remembered Croz's warning as they cautiously moved across the ridge.

"Now", he said, "for something altogether different." The upper part of the north face out on to which the party moved was in some respects the reverse of the one they had left. The east face formed a concave slope, steep above, less steep below. The north face was convex, so that the portion on to which they now moved was inclined at a relatively easy angle; only below did it curl over into the great precipices of the north face, hidden from their sight.

The slope was of a relatively easy angle—less than 40 degrees, Whymper noted. But it is not only the angle that decides the difficulty of a mountain slope. The character of the ground, the ease with which boot nail or finger tip can make suitable contact with the rock is even more important, and it was in this respect that the upper part of the north face presented particular dangers. It was known to the Zermatt men as the Latze Seite or 'false face', a phrase used to describe the sheltered or lee side of a house. The upper part of the north face was just such a place, sheltered by the lie of the land from most of the sun, holding the snow, freezing up easily and remaining frozen when other parts of the mountain were being thawed back to life. Thus what might have been handholds were filled with hard frozen snow; many of the rocks were covered with a thin film of ice; the whole character of what might have been looked on as a reasonably inclined slope thus became, instead, a slippery pathway whose every inch demanded caution. Below and behind, felt more than seen, there dropped away a great void, so that if one looked downwards one saw the rocks a few feet away and then nothing until the slopes of the Matterhorn Glacier, some 4,000 feet below.

The place was dangerous rather than difficult and it was one which any experienced mountaineer would have tackled with little more than the exercise of additional caution. Croz went easily ahead, chipping steps where necessary, scraping away the snow from handholds where this was possible. Occasionally he stopped, one hand grasping a good hold, and turned round to help Whymper. Whymper offered to do the same for Hudson but found that he rarely needed the help; only Hadow, between Hudson and old Peter, was in difficulties, floundering at times,

The upper section of the Hornli Ridge (centre) showing the shoulder above which the party moved onto the North Face and where the fall occurred on the descent

wondering no doubt how long this bad stretch would last, and possibly casting an occasional glance back and down towards the airy spaces below.

The whole party was soon moving across the slippery sloping rock roof of the mountain. At first they traversed out horizontally, taking the easiest route, safeguarding one another where possible by laying the rope behind such small rugosities as the surface afforded. They were soon strung out across the face. It was customary for members of a party to climb far closer together than is the case today, and it seems likely that only 20 feet or so separated each of them, in which case the two 100-foot lengths of Manilla would have been sufficient to link them all, even allowing for the amount used up by waist loops.

They continued horizontally for some 400 feet, silently, concentrating on the task in hand, wondering whether even now all might have been in vain.

Then Croz began to move cautiously upwards. He ascended for some 60 feet, the others strung out behind him, and then began to traverse back leftwards towards the ridge once again. It was still awkward rather than difficult work, but it demanded the utmost care. Everyone moved slowly, one at a time. It was an hour and a half before they reached the ridge once more.

The traverse back ended at an awkward corner, and Croz cautiously edged round it. Whymper followed him. Then the others.

Before their eager eyes there lay a ridge some 200 feet long. But it rose at an easy angle. It was, moreover, a ridge not of rock but of snow up which, they saw at a glance, they could move without trouble. And above and beyond it there stretched only the deep azure blue of a cloudless sky.

Croz was already kicking steps up the slope; the others followed as speedily as possible. It was not fast enough for Croz, or for Whymper. A stretch of snow only three times as long as a cricket pitch separated them from the top of the Matterhorn. And still they did not know whether the Italians had got there first.

They were hampered by the men behind, and as the slope eased off Croz unroped. So did Whymper. So, it is almost certain, did Hudson. Hadow and the others were safe enough at the back.

Then the three men raced for the summit. For once the solemn ritual between employer and employed broke down. Croz of course had worked with Whymper as a companion almost as much as a guide. Hudson, 'almost as good as a guide', was now being treated like one, as the polite convention fell away. Here was no Croz handing his master 'L'Aiguille Verte entièrement et completement'; here was no formal courtesy of 'Vous grimpez comme un chamois, Monsieur'.

It was a measure of the event that the men ran, formalities forgotten. They reached the summit within seconds of one another.

There was no sign of the Italians.

Arriving at the summit. An illusrtation by Gustav Doré

'At 1.40pm the world was at our feet,' wrote Whymper six years later, 'and the Matterhorn was conquered.'

The figures were seen in Zermatt. They were seen at Breuil. They were seen on the Riffelberg where Girdlestone, preparing for an ascent the following day, was looking through his glasses and saw the dash up the final slope, a sight which, as he wrote back to England, 'delighted me immensely and made me enjoy the Mt. Rosa all the more'.

"Croz! Coz! Come here!" Whymper's illustration of arrival at the summit from Scrambles

Yet to Hudson and Whymper and Croz it was not yet certain beyond all doubt that they had forestalled the Italians. The summit ridge of the Matterhorn is a horizontal ridge of rock and snow rather more than 100 yards long. They had arrived at the northern, Swiss, end of the ridge pole, and it was always possible that the Italians had reached and remained at the other end.

As the rest of the party arrived, they hastened along the ridge, looking to right and left for signs of footprints. On all sides the snow was untrodden.

In such illusory moments of victory, men behave in character. Whymper was no exception. Two things moved him—exultation that his party, as he thought of it, had been triumphant, and regret that Carrel was not there with him.

Where, in fact, were the Italians?

Croz and Whymper looked down the Italian slope of the mountain and now saw them. Far away, some 1,250 feet below, there were small dots which moved, if almost imperceptibly, along the ridge.

Whymper, who had seen them first, was to give a graphic account of this moment of personal victory.

"Croz, Croz, come here", he shouted.

"Where are they, monsieur?" asked Croz, hurrying back to where Whymper was excitedly pointing.

"There—don't you see them—down there."

Croz followed the line of the pointing arm, and as he saw the figures, began to estimate their chances of reaching the summit that day. "Ah! the coquins, they are low down", he commented according to Whymper who was by this time intent on making himself seen and heard. "Croz, we must make those fellows hear us", he shouted. For a few moments they bellowed in full throat.

The Italians glanced up, but it was not obvious that the summit party had been seen.

In fact, the small figures outlined against the sky told Carrel all that he needed to know. He had recognised Whymper's white slop trousers and the Italian party halted to discuss what should be done.

On the summit Whymper knew none of this. "Croz, we must make them hear us; they shall hear us!"

He picked up a lump of rock and threw it down the face—well away from the ridge on which the Italians were standing. Croz did the same, and as the rocks thundered down the Italians turned to descend.

Whymper guessed what his old guide must be feeling. 'I would that the leader of that party could have stood with us at that moment,' he thought as he regarded the Italians, 'for our victorious shouts conveyed to him the disappointment of the ambition of a lifetime. He was the man, of all those who attempted the ascent of the Matterhorn, who most deserved to be the first upon its summit. He was the first to doubt its inaccessibility, and he was the only man who persisted in believing that its ascent would be accomplished. It was the aim of his life to make the ascent from the side of Italy, for the honour of his native valley. For a time he had the game in his hands; he played it as he thought best; but he made a false move, and he lost it.'

It was indeed an occasion of occasions. The most famous summit of the Alps had at last been climbed. The two finest amateurs then alive had taken part in the ascent. Fate had even organised the moment so that the Italians could be seen in their defeat. She had also organised much else.

On the summit everyone was exultant; each man had his own version of how they should celebrate their success when they got back to Zermatt that night. Hudson wondered whether M'Cormick had eventually arrived, and grieved for the chance of the great adventure that his friend had missed. Whymper and Douglas may have felt much the same about Girdlestone. After all, young Hadow had successfully scrambled to the top without disaster and there seemed little doubt that Girdlestone could have done the same. There was also Robertson, whom Hudson had met in Chamonix; Kennedy who might also have shared their victory; and Birkbeck who might have been one of the party if illness had not forced him back to England.

The guides, too, were in high spirits. For Croz it was a great day, crowning his long association with Whymper even if he was in fact employed by Hudson. As for the Taugwalders, their feelings were expressed by young Peter—'My heart was so light that I could have taken wing, far away and out across all the mountains, heaven knows where to—down to my sweetheart in Zermatt, perhaps.'

Only Croz had perhaps a suspicion of worry. Whymper noted that they had come up rather slowly, and the guide commented: "Yes, I would rather go down with you and another guide alone than with those who are going." It seems, as Whymper quotes it, a strange remark for the guide of one man to make to another; yet the friendship between Whymper and Croz was of long standing and as firm as all friendships wrought in dangerous places.

Croz and Whymper went back to the northern end of the ridge where the rest of the party were now unpacking the food. Croz took the tent-pole and triumphantly plunged it down into the snow. One can imagine the reaction. "Fine. There is the flag pole, but where is the flag?"

The guide smiled knowingly and began to undo the blue smock which he had bought in Martigny a few days previously. "Here it is", he answered, attaching it to the pole.

There was not a breath of wind. The smock hung limply down. But it was seen in Zermatt. It was seen at Breuil where poor Favre took it as proof that Carrel had succeeded. It was seen on the Riffel Alp where men looked at one another almost disbelieving, not a few of them tut-tutting and enquiring what the world was coming to. They had reason on their side. The six-foot length of wood with its few yards of rough fabric marked the end of one age and the beginning of another as surely as the thunder of the guns at Valmy. There Kellerman had shown that the armies of the republic could stand firm against the assaults of the old order; here men had shown that even the most formidable mountains, with their legendary barricades, their ghosts and their mysteries, could be subdued by all-conquering enlightened man. At least, that was what they appeared to have shown.

Whymper now went to the highest point on the ridge and broke off the real physical summit of the Matterhorn, a small pyramid of mica schist as big as a cricket ball which repeats in micro scale many features of the mountain itself. He put the rock in his rucksack and joined the others.

More than one of the men almost certainly breathed the words "What a day!" It was so still that Croz could light his pipe without difficulty. There were no clouds, not a tatter of mist. It was one of those rare occasions when the sky has that deep azure quality of outer space, when the most minute detail of rock and ice is etched diamond-hard as far as the horizon. The Maritime Alps, 130 miles away, could be clearly seen; so could the great peaks of the Dauphiné, among them the Pelvoux on whose flanks Whymper had first climbed into Alpine fame only four brief years ago. The huge bulk of the Ecrins reared up like the side of a white whale and Croz and Whymper must have remembered with satisfaction how they had beaten it into submission almost exactly a year previously. To the west Mont Blanc, as ever the obvious monarch of them all, glowed in the sunshine, while to the north, across the deep trench of the Rhone, there rose the great peaks of the Oberland. Away to the east, peak led the eye to ever diminishing peak, immense in numbers, infinite in variety.

To the south, stretching beyond the pastures of Breuil, 8,000 feet below, there lay the mysteries of Italy. 'There were forests black and gloomy and meadows bright and lively,' wrote Whymper, 'bounding waterfalls and tranquil lakes; fertile lands and savage wastes; sunny plains and frigid plateaux. There were the most rugged forms, and the most graceful outlines—bold, perpendicular cliffs, and gentle, undulating slopes; rocky mountains and snowy mountains, sombre and solemn, or glittering and white, with walls—turrets—pinnacles—pyramids—domes—cones and spires! There was every combination that the world can give, and every contrast that the heart could desire.'

It was a moment never to forget.

They had all unroped, and the coils lay curled on the snow as they built the traditional cairn, prising loose the rocks from beneath the snow. Then they rested and ate, drank or sketched, peered over the tremendous precipices which fell from their ridge pole in space, and basked in their victory.

They spent an hour on the summit. Then they prepared for the descent.

Chapter eight

DESCENT

I T WAS ABOUT 2.45PM WHEN THE FOUR AMATEURS, the two Valaisans and the solitary Savoyard left the summit of the Matterhorn. The vital details of exactly what took place during the ten minutes or so before they left must be inferred. Whymper's account, the only one ever given, is brief and somewhat vague over the things that matter. This is natural enough. The confusion that is apt to accompany great victory is historically tantalising but very frequent. The blood was still coursing more quickly than usual through the veins of the victors; and, after all, what reason was there for noting and remembering everything? Captain Farrar, a later and discerning mountaineer and a President of the Alpine Club, made the point when he wrote to Coolidge, the great Alpine historian. 'Who on earth in those early days ever expected the minute criticism to which nowadays Alpine matters are, in the fierce light of completed knowledge, exposed?' he asked. 'God help all those early authors. . . .'

Soon after 2.30pm, thoughts were put into words and one of the party, probably Michel Croz, must have faced them with things to come.

"Gentlemen, we had better be moving."

How were they to go down? Who was to lead? Who was to occupy the responsible position of last man, sheet-anchor of the whole rope?

Hudson looked across to Whymper who was still sketching. "Croz had better go first", he said. Hadow could come next while Hudson himself would be third on the rope. If his ability gave him, in effect, professional status, there would be guide, amateur, guide, then Lord Francis Douglas behind as the next amateur. The two Taugwalders and Whymper could bring up the rear.

In the circumstances it seemed almost unnecessary to worry about such things. A party which could succeed on the Matterhorn was hardly the sort to need ordinary rules. There was not the slightest chance of the weather breaking. For six of the men the ascent had been almost ludicrously well within their capacities. Young Hadow of course had not been happy; he had been slipping about a good deal, but between two experienced men not even that need be dangerous.

Then they remembered the bad bit, the shaded roof of the mountain. Why not, Whymper suggested to Hudson, attach a fixed rope at the top of that stretch? It was the sensible sort of thing that Whymper would think of. He had no inhibitions about using grapnels, pitons, any 'mechanical' device to hand it if helped in the ascent or descent of a mountain. A fixed rope would give them just that extra bit of security.

According to Whymper, Hudson 'approved the plan, but it was not definitely settled that it should be done'. It is possible that Hudson's agreement was grudging. It is possible that Whymper's phrase is merely another indication of that rough treatment which in the aftermath of events he was apt to give Hudson. It is possible that in such glorious and confident circumstances no one thought it necessary to lay hold of the suggestion.

As they were talking, Croz went to the ropes. There were four of them, it will be remembered—the two 100-foot lengths of Manilla with which they had been tied during the ascent; the 150 feet of stouter rope, apt to be slightly heavy in use; and the sash line, more than 200 feet of it.

The 150 feet of heavy stuff was in the nature of a spare and Croz picked it up as such and probably strapped it to his load. This left the two lengths of Manilla and the sash line. Having tied on to one of the 100-foot lengths, Croz began to rope up Hadow, Hudson and Lord Francis Douglas in that order. Young Peter, somewhat casually given pride of place as last man of the party, was about to tie himself on to the end of the second 100-foot length. Croz meanwhile began to prospect the route down.

Whymper was still sketching a hundred feet or more away as young

Peter went across to him and prepared to tie him on, before linking both of them, via his father, to the rest of the party. Then someone remembered the names.

The names in the bottle. Together with the erection of a summit cairn, putting the names in a bottle formed part of the ritual of mountaineering, as inseparable from a successful first ascent as was the roar of the miniature cannon which for more than half a century greeted each successful party on Mont Blanc as it entered the village street of Chamonix.

Whymper still had his sketching pad out and his companions shouted along to him. Right. He would do the bottle business. They could start moving off and he would catch them up. He went along and young Peter followed him, rope in hand.

At the best point on the ridge, Croz was already at the top of the rocks leading down. Hadow and Hudson and Douglas had tightened their boot laces, checked that they had left nothing on the summit, and were also ready to move off.

Behind Douglas, only a few yards from him, stood old Peter, knowing it was right that he should tie on to Douglas, his employer, and not wait for Whymper and his son. Most of the first 100-foot length of Manilla had been used up in tying the first four members of the party. What remained was inadequate for a fifth man unless he were to tie on far nearer to the fourth man than was considered safe. The second 100-foot length was with Whymper and his son.

Old Peter unslung 30 feet or so of the sash line and with it linked himself to Douglas. He could keep the Englishman on a tight rope if necessary. The stuff was not as thick as the Manilla; but it was rope, and the men who had made such a business of mountain climbing during the last decade or so had always stressed the importance of rope. Taugwalder, like most guides of the period, knew little of breaking strains, of the weaknesses produced by knots, of the limitations inherent in this cord in which men now seemed to have such trust. In its own way, rope of any sort had become almost a talisman, a lucky charm, a protection against all disaster, a physical Cross which warded off evil much as making the Sign would keep the spirits at bay in the lonely watches of the night. Old Peter tied on to Douglas quite happily, warned over his shoulder that his son should not waste too much time, and shouted down to Croz that he was now ready to move off.

Whymper finished writing the names of the seven men, tore the sheet from his little three-by-four sketch pad, rolled it quickly, stuck it in one of the bottles they had emptied, and pushed the bottle well into the foot of the cairn.

He straightened himself and turned to young Peter, who had by this time tied himself securely to one end of the 100-foot length and who now handed the rest to Whymper. The Englishman tied himself on, leaving some 20 to 30 feet between himself and the guide. The waist-loops had used some 10 feet and the remainder Whymper now coiled across his shoulders in the easy way of a guide.

He took one last look along that narrow ridge of snow whose attainment had been his aim for years. Except for young Peter he was now utterly alone. The five other members of the party had by this time disappeared down and over on to the face of the mountain. They were quite out of sight but there came up through the still air an occasional word of advice or caution, clearly heard yet curiously disjointed, as though from another world.

Otherwise all was silent.

Whymper and young Peter turned to follow them. Whymper later wrote that they 'ran down', an understandable over statement that stresses the different qualities of a rope of two agile experienced men and a rope with five of more mixed experience.

They caught up with their companions just as the latter had reached the upper rocks of the difficult stretch. Here the snow gave out on to ice-clad rocks. You could see them stretching downwards for a few hundred feet, interspersed by minor and usually iced protruberances; the ground was broken but it was not broken in a way which makes for ease or safety. There were few spikes, pinnacles, solid bollards, around which a man might belay a rope as a precaution; instead, the feeling which the terrain gave was one of smoothness, roundness. Even though the angle was not excessive it gave an air of insecurity. Below it, moreover, the rocks steepened and curled over to the great void below.

Whymper noticed that no fixed rope had been attached to the rocks—possibly because the exact line of descent chosen by Croz passed no suitable place, possibly because Croz had felt in a moment of weak judgment that it was not really necessary. Whymper noticed also the immense difference between the ascent of such a place, facing in, only dimly aware of the great gulf below, and its descent, facing out, constantly presented with the possibilities of a slip.

Below him, each member of the party seemed well aware of the situation. Croz would move on a few feet and then turn to help Hadow down the rocks as Hudson carefully paid out the rope, keeping it as taut as possible, doing his best to brace himself for the shock that would come if Hadow slipped. Then Hudson would move, sure of himself and hardly needing the protection of the rope which Douglas paid out with the ability of a man who was familiar with the technique. Last of all came old Peter, also quite sure of himself, taking in the spare rope as he moved from step to step, then calling down that he was secure, and occasionally giving Croz a word of advice about the rocks that were immediately ahead and which he could see slightly better from his higher position.

It was now almost 3pm, and for some minutes Whymper and young Peter followed the others without a word, closing up to the older guide until they were only some 20 feet or so from him.

They moved thus for some way, still not speaking. Then Douglas looked back. He may have seen that Hadow, next but one in front of him, was having trouble. He may have been impressed by the exposure of the place. He may have felt uneasy about his ability to hold Hudson should even Hudson slip.

And now his instinct for command came uppermost.

Douglas looked back to Whymper and suggested that Taugwalder should tie on to Whymper and his son. That, after all, was how they had intended to descend, as one roped party. That, so far as Douglas knew, was the way the matter should be handled, and it was time for someone to say so—even though Hudson in front of him appeared not to worry, even though Whymper above had said nothing.

It was, he felt, the right thing to do, and doing it must have been one of the most morally courageous acts of Douglas's life. To admit that he would be happier for greater aid showed, in this situation, the character of the man who is strong enough to turn back when judgment says that it is necessary.

In Whymper's words, Douglas asked him "to tie on to old Peter, as he feared, he said, that Taugwalder would not be able to hold his ground if a slip occurred". If he did, in fact, use the words that Whymper infers, he must have been remarkably unheeding of their effect on the other members of the party, and it seems more likely that he merely asked Whymper to tie on, and left the implication as merely an implication.

Assuming, as all did, that one rope of seven was safer than two ropes of five and of two, the request to tie on should have come from Hudson, from Whymper, from Croz, even from Taugwalder. It is difficult not to think that for a moment command of the party had been firmly taken by the man best fitted by instinct, if not by experience, to exercise it. Yet Douglas was still only 18.

Whymper agreed. He closed up as far as was convenient, then let down to old Peter the unused portion of the 100-foot length of Manilla which until now had been slung across his shoulders. Old Peter tied on.

Now they were really one confident party again, as they had been coming up. Only the rest of the difficult stretch remained. It would soon be over. There would be nothing more to worry about and if they hurried they would be down in Zermatt soon after dusk.

In the light of modern experience, one thing was wrong. It would, naturally enough, have been impossible for Whymper to refuse to tie on to the lower party in such circumstances. But on a slope where there are few suitable belays, where there is doubt that one man may be able to hold another, adding two men to a party of five merely compounds the dangers. They were now, it is true, one confident party again. But each was comparatively defenceless against the results of a serious slip made by any of the other six.

They moved on downwards in silence. The only sounds to be heard were the chink of metal as ice axe swung against the slope, the soft crunch as boot settled down to snow-filled hold, the rasp of nail against rock. Far away the peaks shone in the afternoon sunlight.

Immediately in front the rocks curled over into space and the eye met nothing more until it rested on the Matterhorn Glacier, more than three quarters of a mile below, its huge crevasses transformed to a mere tracery of lines.

They were moving cautiously, one at a time, and at the rear of the party Whymper and the Taugwalders could see little of what was happening ahead and below. They waited their turn and they may even have felt a little impatient.

Then, in an instant, all was changed.

Their reflexes operated. They were clinging to the rocks with the rope taut between them.

Below, slipping down on their backs, their hands desperately trying to grasp something and helplessly scrabbling against the rocks, were their four companions, Croz, Hadow, Hudson and Lord Francis Douglas.

Old Peter was lucky. Slightly above him there lay a large rock, securely part of the mountain. He turned to it, grasped it with both arms, automatically taking in the slack between Whymper and himself.

Whymper, though less well-placed, had reacted as quickly, and so had young Peter, higher up the face. Certainly between old Peter and Whymper, probably between Whymper and young Peter, the rope was taut, and the shock of the falling bodies below was taken by them as one man.

The rope between Douglas and old Peter whipped through the guide's hands, leaving a searing mark that was to remain for weeks. Then it snapped taut with a sound that Whymper was to remember for a quarter of a century. The rope broke in midair.

'For a few seconds', Whymper later wrote, 'we saw our unfortunate companions sliding downwards on their backs, and spreading out their hands, endeavouring to save themselves. They passed from our sight uninjured, disappeared one by one, and fell from precipice to precipice on to the Matterhorn-gletscher below, a distance of nearly 4,000 feet in height.'

Following them there went the chatter of small and yet smaller stones, coasting down the slope and skimming out into space. Then there was silence once more.

For half an hour neither Whymper nor the Taugwalders moved. Paralysing shock, and fear, had taken over. 'We could hardly move for a while, so terrified were we', said young Peter later. Whymper claimed that the two guides, 'paralysed by terror, cried like infants'. Young Peter recorded that Whymper 'was trembling so violently that he could hardly manage a safe step forward'. Both statements were made with ill grace, each possibly an effort to brush off on to others some of the odium that the disaster created. It seems likely that Whymper kept his head better than did the guides. But it would, after all, have been no reflection on any man had he been distraught.

Nervous reaction could hardly have come in a worse place. 'Knee-dissolving fear', the trembling of the muscles, the inability to place feet firmly—all these were the natural and inevitable responses to the sight of their four companions sliding helplessly to their deaths. They made every move a dangerous one on a slope where firmness was all.

When they found their voices, old Peter could only stammer over and over again: "Chamonix; what will Chamonix say?" an instinctive indication that he knew how difficult it would be for Savoyards to believe that the masterly Croz had been involved in such a disaster. Young Peter's cry of "We are lost! We are lost!" was soon taken up by his father—according to Whymper, who lost no opportunity of describing the behaviour of the Taugwalders in the blackest possible terms.

The reason for this attitude, which was to run like a dark line through much of Whymper's subsequent life, is explained if not justified by the events of the next few moments.

Gustav Doré's famous illustration of the accident

Old Peter at last changed his stance and belayed himself securely. His son then began to climb cautiously down. Whymper did the same and the three of them were soon standing together.

Whymper acted immediately. He examined the rope which had snapped in midair. And he found to his horror that it was not the thickest of his ropes, not the 150-foot length which would have been long enough to link the five leading men, not the Manilla, but part of the long coil of weaker rope still coiled around old Peter's shoulders.

In the confused aftermath of tragedy, Whymper, only 25, relatively inexperienced in the ways of the world, could hardly be expected to think clearly about the situation back on the summit half an hour previously. He could hardly be expected to remember the details. It was natural enough that there should flash into his mind the thought that old Peter might have used the thinnest rope deliberately, as a safeguard, as an insurance against a slip by the men in front of him.

There is no doubt that such thoughts were completely unjustified. The confusing and unorganised roping-up of a virtually leaderless party on the summit provided, as Whymper must have admitted had he thought about it, sufficient explanation for the choice. It is easy to write 'fatal choice'. But it must be remembered that had another rope been used the likelihood is that the whole party of seven would have been pulled to destruction. Unless, that is, old Peter, clinging to his rock, had been able to withstand the pull of four falling men. Also it must be remembered that it was rope 'of a kind that I used formerly' as Whymper himself put it.

As he and the two guides stood in the afternoon sunlight, the possibilities of accusation were obvious. 'I saw at once that a serious question was involved, and made him give me the end', Whymper later wrote.

What he did not explain was just what he meant by the words. Whymper's 'made him give me the end' may have meant that he took the end of the 200-foot length from old Peter, satisfied himself that it had broken in midair and had not been previously tampered with, and then handed it back to the guide who recoiled it over his shoulder. But the phrase 'made him give me the end' might well suggest something different. The three men were shortly afterwards cutting off numerous lengths of this line and securing them to the rocks as fixed ropes. And it seems possible that on Whymper's instructions, Taugwalder took out his knife, cut the rope a foot or so from the broken end, and handed this portion to Whymper who stowed it away in his rucksack.

They were still on the steep 'roof'. It was by this time about four o'clock, and it was essential to move. Whymper's German was very slight, as was young Peter's French. Even in different circumstances conversation would not have been easy, but in his blunt way Whymper no doubt showed that he looked on the elder guide as at least morally responsible for what had happened. 'For more than two hours afterwards', he wrote of the journey which now started, 'I thought every moment that the next would be my last; for the Taugwalders, utterly unnerved, were not only incapable of giving assistance, but were in such a state that a slip might have been expected from one or the other at any moment. I do the younger man, moreover, no injustice when I say that immediately we got to the easy part of the descent he was able to laugh, smoke, and eat as if nothing had happened.' No doubt the Taugwalders were unnerved. But there is a sneer in the words that was to harm Edward Whymper almost as much as it harmed the Taugwalders.

There is a phrase, 'a nightmare journey', which is too frequently glibly used to describe situations that are little more than difficult and slightly dangerous. It can be used with justification of the passage down the remaining few hundred feet of steep rock on which Whymper and the Taugwalders now started. Only those who have been forced by unexpected circumstance to move over such a distance, knowing that each move may be fatal and that each move must be made, can perhaps understand the tumult in the minds of all three men. It can come on mountains; it can come on minefields; it can come in weapon disposal, and in each case survival is the one undeniable proof that muscle and brain, nerve and mind, their collaboration tested as in few other conditions, have still continued to do their combined task.

With Whymper and the Taugwalders, the thin links held, in spite of the strain provided more by the memory of their comrades sliding helplessly to death than by the physical difficulty of the rocks. The thin links held. And it is difficult, therefore, not to believe that some iron in the spirit kept all three men rather more in check than any of their subsequent stories would lead one to believe. Old Peter, according to his son, 'climbed on in front, continually turning back to place Whymper's legs on the broken ledges of rock'. According to Whymper, 'the men were afraid to proceed, and several times old Peter turned with ashy face and faltering limbs, and said, with terrible emphasis, "I cannot!" Maybe. But they could; and they did.

Wherever a suitable rock protruded, old Peter would cut a length of the sash line, deftly loop it round the rock, knot it firmly, and then wriggle it with his hand so that it hung down the route he was to take. For each man in succession it provided an additional safeguard, something to be grasped securely if for an instant one felt the foot slipping.

It was slow going, heavier on the nerves than on the wind. 'We had to stop over and again to rest, for our spirits were low indeed', young Peter said, and although the difficult stretch was only a matter of some few hundred feet, it was six o'clock before the three men arrived at last on the relatively flat snow slope of the Shoulder. Here the worst of the tension relaxed.

On the Shoulder they found their rucksacks, their provisions, and what Whymper calls 'the little effects of those who were lost', all of which they had left in such high spirits some seven hours previously. From here they could look out across the steep slopes of the north face and all three began to scan them for signs of their comrades. It is not at all certain what they saw. A week later in Zermatt Whymper said that they had seen two ice axes smashed in—'enfoncées'—the snow of the north face, and he repeated the statement a few days later. Writing to *The Times* in August, he said that he had looked 'frequently, but in vain, for traces of my unfortunate companions'. Young Peter claimed years later, however, that they saw 'far down below . . . our poor comrades lying on the cold glacier'. The likeliest thing is that they saw what at a distance they believed were axes; and that Whymper, thinking over the matter later, decided that they were probably wrong.

It was now four hours since they had eaten, and they opened the rucksacks. Young Peter summed up their feelings when he recorded that they 'tried to eat a little, but found it difficult to swallow a morsel; we felt as if our gullets had been tied with a cord'. They ate what they could; then they got ready to continue the descent.

Whymper's illustration of the fog bow seen by the survivors which appeared in Scrambles

As they were preparing to move off, they halted. For to the south-east, seen across the Furgg Glacier as they looked towards the peaks of Monte Rosa, there appeared an amazing spectacle. 'Lo! a mighty arch appeared, rising above the Lyskamm, high into the sky', Whymper later wrote. 'Pale, colourless, and noiseless, but perfectly sharp and defined, except where it was lost in the clouds, this unearthly apparition seemed like a vision from another world; and, almost appalled, we watched with amazement the gradual development of two vast crosses, one on either side. If the Taugwalders had not been the first to perceive it, I should have doubted my senses. They thought it had some connection with the accident, and I, after a while, that it might bear some relation to ourselves. But our movements had no effect upon it. The spectral forms remained motionless. It was a fearful and wonderful sight; unique in my experience, and impressive beyond description, coming at such a moment.'

Impressive, that is, according to Whymper as he recounted the incident a few years later when writing his famous book. Yet he appears not to have mentioned the spectacle at all in the statements which he made during the next few days to Girdlestone; to the English Chaplain at Geneva who came up to Zermatt; to the Rev. M'Cormick, or to the Rev. William Prior, another Englishman passing through the village to whom he gave a graphic account of the descent. He did not mention it at the enquiry which was held in Zermatt and he did not mention it in the letter which he eventually wrote to *The Times*. 'Certainly, I, for one, never saw anything of the three [sic] crosses', young Peter later declared.

Here, as Sir Charles Snow has said of the differing evidence which he and others have presented of the great pre-war radar controversy, 'It might seem that the collision is head on. Who is wrong? Whose memory is defective? Where is the contradiction?'

And, as in that later unmatching up of the evidence, one can reply as Snow did to his own rhetorical question. 'The answer is undramatic and something of an anticlimax. No one is wrong. No one's memory is defective. There is no contradiction.'

To understand how this is so, it is necessary to remember that Whymper was to draw a dramatic and magnificent full page illustration of the crosses for the *Scrambles*; one of the illustrations which, as he put it in a letter to a friend, 'will contain enough sensations for half a dozen volumes'. One of these illustrations showed a celebrated incident on the Ecrins which, it was later claimed, had never taken place. Neither side won a clear victory in the argument which ensued over that particular discrepancy, but an illuminating comment on it was made by Captain Farrar. 'I do not think W[hymper] *invented* the incident', he wrote to the Rev. W. A. B. Coolidge. 'Remember he became a noted man through the Matterhorn affair. He was writing his first book, which was looked for by the public and was expected to be sensational. What more natural than that a clever draughtsman should use some little incident to make a sensational picture and unconsciously exaggerate? We are all human.'

This was Farrar's comment on the famous 'Almer's Leap' controversy and it seems probable that it could have been made just as accurately of Whymper's illustration showing the crosses in the sky. He did not invent it, even though he probably strayed rather near that borderline which separates fact and fiction. After all, all three men were strung to a high pitch of tension. After all, recalling history in the calm is difficult, and it would be easy enough to recall a minor incident and, like Henry's fighters of St. Crispian's day, 'remember with advantages'. After all, in Farrar's understanding phrase, we are all human.

Whatever the exact truth of the matter, Whymper and the guides were still high on the mountain at the time of the incident. Only some three hours of light remained; they had little protection; they would have to descend as far as possible before nightfall. However, before they moved off, the two Taugwalders exchanged a few words in patois which Whymper could not understand.

Then young Peter turned to him. Whymper made no reference either at the enquiry at Zermatt or in his subsequent letter to *The Times* to the traumatic incident which followed. His version, written some years later and given in the *Scrambles* is clear and uncompromising. "We are poor men", he has young Peter saying. "We have lost our Herr; we shall not get paid; we can ill afford this." Whymper stopped him, saying that that was nonsense. "I shall pay you, of course, just as if your Herr were here."

Once again, according to Whymper, the two men spoke together. Then, again according to Whymper, young Peter explained. "We don't wish you to pay us. We wish you to write in the hotel book at Zermatt, and to your journals, that we have not been paid." The explanation was forthcoming when Whymper asked what he meant. "Why, next year there will be many travellers at Zermatt, and we shall get more voyageurs."

This damning accusation against the Taugwalders has for years been known as Whymper's main account of the incident. In fact he gave a version in Zermatt, a few days after the accident, which was recorded by the Rev. W. Prior, who passed it on in a letter to his old friend, Mr. Mackenzie, the British Consul in Geneva. This letter throws fresh light on what the Taugwalders actually said and—just as important—it helps to explain both Whymper's subsequent reluctance to give his own account of the accident, and his indictment of the Taugwalders when he eventually did so.

'I am much disgusted with the conduct of the Taugwalders pere & fils,' wrote Prior. 'An hour after the accident they bothered Whymper to know who was to pay them, and asked him to send an account to the Newspapers mentioning their names, in order that among travellers they might have next year *a success de curiosite*.'

This version, which was obtained within four days of the accident at least through, and probably directly from, Whymper reveals a flinty and somewhat peasant attitude to the main chance, yet it reveals something slightly different from what Whymper implied six years later. It is possible that the Taugwalders did, in fact, suggest that Whymper should spread a 'non-payment' story, but it has always seemed singularly out-of-character. If this was the case, moreover, it seems curious that Prior did not know of it and pass on the information to the British Consul. It seems only possible to conclude that when Whymper wrote the original memorandum on which he later drew for his story, the facts, which in view of the language difficulties must have been confused enough in the first place, were further distorted by the vagaries of memory. The process is familiar enough.

Prior's statement that the Taugwalders hoped for more business merely by the mention of their names does make one thing much more understandable. This is Whymper's subsequent, and almost pathological, reluctance to describe what had happened. Almost any description would, inevitably, publicise the work of the Taugwalders.

On the mountain, all of them were wrought up. They did not speak a common language. And it seems unlikely that Whymper had more than a general idea of what the Taugwalders were in fact suggesting. It was, however, enough to set him off down the cliffs in a rage; moving, as he himself put it, so 'recklessly', that he brought protests from the guides.

All three of them still hoped that they might get off the rocks, or at least the worst of them, by the time it was dark. Yet easy as the route now was by comparison with the nightmare passage of the 'roof' above, it was yet dangerous enough. All three men were sufficiently experienced to know that on any mountain constant vigilance is the price of survival. There was a certain maximum speed they could not safely exceed, and in the failing light they realised they would not reach Zermatt that night. The twilight crept up, past and over them, and they went on through the dimming light and deepening shadows of what had been a splendid day.

At last they could go on no longer. In spite of the stars, it was too dark to move in such a place with safety, and they picked the best situation they could find, a slab of rock which could hold, but only just hold, the three of them. There they lay down to get what rest they could, Whymper keeping aloof from the two guides.

Luckily, the weather held. Even so, it was a wretched enough night, and at 3.30am they were on their way down again, still hurrying, on tracks, keeping unspoken at the back of their minds, the lingering but grotesque hope that one or more of their companions might even have survived the terrible fall and might be rescued if they moved fast enough.

About their arrival back in Zermatt, a sizeable village even a century ago, there hangs a contradictory confusion of evidence. Whymper says that they got back at 10.30pm. Girdlestone says it was 2.00pm—after lunch in other words. Young Peter says it was 3.00pm; while Miss Brevoort, an American woman just starting her climbing career and hearing an account of the disaster in the Monte Rosa only a few weeks later, quotes the maid who had seen the three men arrive 'late on Saturday night'. It seems certain, in fact, that Whymper and the two Taugwalders were back in Zermatt before midday; the exact hour is unimportant—but it demonstrates the conflict of evidence which surrounds some of the simplest, and presumably most checkable, facts.

There had been some anxiety in the village when no one had returned on the Friday night. Yet they might, after all, have reached one of the upper chalets late and then slept there, exhausted with success, before completing their return journey.

Now only three came back. Seiler was waiting at the door of the Monte Rosa. In silence he followed Whymper up to his room, unwilling at first to ask the obvious question and to receive the obvious answer. In the room, as Whymper turned to him, he at last demanded: "What is the matter?"

"The Taugwalders and I have returned," Whymper replied.

PART FOUR
THE AFTERMATH

Chapter nine

Search

MOUNTAINEERING ACCIDENTS INVARIABLY touch a hard note of tragedy curiously different from that produced by death in other places. Here it marks down so frequently the young, the active, the daring. The magnificence of the mountains contrasts so strongly with the shattered bodies. Often, moreover, there is the haunting knowledge that the border between survival and disaster was so easily avoidable: the foot planted a fraction of an inch to left or right; a hold tested with the subconscious momentary tension that must, on this one fatal occasion, have been lacking; the belay taken even though commonsense had suggested no real necessity—these are the minute watersheds dividing life from death. Even today, even after Auschwitz, even after Hiroshima, death in the mountains still strikes with a bitter insistence that something personal has unnecessarily been snatched away. A century and a half ago, human life might be more brutish, more short and more mean than it is today, yet it still had a higher value and mountain tragedy carried a greater quality of regret. Four men killed in a single moment on a single mountain! This alone would have been enough to send a shudder through the civilised world, even had the disaster not happened on the Matterhorn, even had there not been a suggestion of international rivalry, even had one of those who fell not been an English milord. All this combined to give a sensational news worthiness to the disaster which from Saturday, July 15th, spread out from Zermatt in ever-widening ripples.

The village was linked to the outside world neither by carriage-track nor by telegraph and none of the Swiss papers thought it worthwhile to retain even a part time correspondent there. However, at Randa, seven miles down the Vispthal, there lived the local correspondent of the *Journal de Genève* to whom the news filtered down. The first message said only that the mountain had been climbed. News of the disaster came later, and it came with inaccuracies that were to confuse a situation already amply provided with chances for confusion. For the message which made its way out to the world via Randa and the *Journal de Genève* described the order of descent as being Croz leading, followed by Lord Francis Douglas, Hadow, Hudson, Whymper, young Peter Taugwalder and old Peter, in that order; it had Lord Douglas slipping and causing the accident; and it had the rope breaking between Whymper and young Peter. Part of the confusion probably arose from the fact that at times his companions possibly referred to Hadow by his Christian name of Douglas; it would be quickly bruited abroad that the most inexperienced of the two men still in their teens had slipped; and it was natural if unfortunate that two and two should be put together to implicate Lord Francis Douglas. All this would have been straightened out more simply had it not been for the accretions of rumour, gossip, libel and accusation which began to grow around the news as it spread across Europe. Much of this was perhaps inevitable. Even in recounting the simple straight forward story of a single uncomplicated incident, there are enough chances of grasping the wrong end of the stick. Here the sole survivors of the most sensational mountaineering accident of its decade consisted of two guides, one of whom felt himself wrongly placed under suspicion and a young Englishman, inexperienced in the ways of the world, who believed that the best course was to say as little as possible.

If any single cause was responsible for the grotesque growth of rumours it was Whymper's silence. Yet this was natural enough. Few men can have felt more utterly alone than the young Edward Whymper, only 25, surrounded by those whose first language was not his own, involved as he was quick enough to realise in the multitudinous small after-details of death. Seiler had burst into tears on hearing Whymper's news. Whymper himself managed to retain that iron calm which in after years was to give him some of that rocky quality of the mountains themselves.

"Send a man to whoever is concerned," he almost certainly said. "Tell him that we must have as many guides as possible out immediately on the Matterhorn Glacier. There's always a chance . . ." Even Whymper's voice must have trailed off as he tried to convince Seiler as well as himself, that anyone could have survived such an accident.

In Seiler's mind, the mechanics of the matter had already been set in motion. The President of the Commune would officially have to be informed. He would have to raise whatever men were available. There would have to be an enquiry. Mr. Whymper would have to be told, if he did not already know, that he must remain in Zermatt until it was concluded. There would be the bodies, if they could be found, and the funeral, and no doubt the relatives. Behind his grief, one part of Seiler's brain was functioning automatically, operating unemotionally, geared to do the right thing, think of all eventualities, by long years of experience.

Whymper had no such advantage. Far from home, unused to tragedy, he showed more confidence than he felt. Girdlestone, he learned from Seiler, had gone up to the Gornergrat on the Thursday after the party had left for the Matterhorn; had returned to Zermatt on the Friday; and had left later in the day for the Riffelberg. He would now, Seiler added, be somewhere on Monte Rosa.

There was, however, the Reverend Joseph M'Cormick who had arrived on the Friday with Mr. Campbell. They had set off only a short while ago for the Gornergrat, but would be coming back that evening.

Whymper asked Seiler for some note paper. 'My dear Sir—I am told you are a friend of the Rev. C. Hudson, who was with me yesterday on the Matterhorn,' he quickly wrote on it. 'I regret most deeply to say that an accident has occurred to him—I am afraid a fatal one. A party of guides has been sent immediately from here to search for him, and I follow them; but I wish particularly to have an Englishman with me, and I therefore beg, if you can possibly return here by 4.30pm, to do so in order to go with me—I am, my dear Sir, yours very truly, Edward Whymper.' He folded it, addressed it to M'Cormick, and asked Seiler to send it up to the Gornergrat as quickly as possible.

As soon as he could, he added, he himself would follow the guides who would soon be leaving the village on their search for the bodies.

Seiler dissuaded; kindly, understanding Seiler. He knew that the young man would have enough to handle within the next few days; he reminded him that he must be almost at the end of his tether, persuaded him that he could do nothing to help, and almost insisted that the windows be shaded and that he lie down for a few hours rest. Whymper, not a man easily to be persuaded against his will, finally agreed.

Meanwhile, a string of about a score of guides was leaving the village. It was not certain whether the bodies would be accessible. It was not even certain that they would be discovered, since there was always the chance that they might have lodged somewhere high up on the 4,000-foot face. The first thing, therefore, was to reconnoitre, to get some idea of the problems involved.

The men therefore made for the Hohlicht heights, rising above the Zmuttbach which runs into Zermatt from the west. From here they would be able to look across the deep trench of the upper valley, across the nose of the Zmutt Glacier itself, and on to the plateau of the Matterhorn Glacier. The distance to the lower crags of the Matterhorn which rose above the glacier was only some three miles and through the glasses it would be possible to see all that was needed.

It was an unpleasant task. The men moved without speaking, and they made little comment when, only a short way out of the village, they saw a sizeable party approaching them. It consisted of Yeats Browne who had ascended Mont Blanc on the same day as Hudson, Kennedy and young Hadow; the Rev. James Robertson, who only ten days earlier had been asked by Hudson to join him in his Matterhorn attempt; and two other masters from Rugby who had joined Robertson at Chamonix, the Rev. J. S. Philpotts and Mr. Knyvett Wilson. With Franz Andermatten, Jean Tairraz of Chamonix and Frederic Payot, they had taken the High Level route, finally crossed the Col de Valpelline and made their way down the Zmutt Glacier towards Zermatt.

Early that morning they had been puzzled. 'We were ... immediately below the Matterhorn, and observed, with our glasses, what appeared to be a *stone man* on its summit,' Yeats Browne later recorded. 'But inasmuch as the Matterhorn was inaccessible we were obliged to admit that it was a rocky tooth or *dent*, very much like a stone man.' Neither to Yeats Browne, nor to Robertson, nor in fact to any of the others, did it seem likely that the Matterhorn could have been climbed.

Yeats Browne was now walking first down the path, and looked up to greet the long line of sombre men coming towards them. They passed without a word, and he was about to comment on this to Payot, when one of the Zermatt men called back. Browne and those with him did not hear the words, but those behind stopped to talk to the guides. Then they hurried on to tell Browne the news. It had indeed been a stone man. The Matterhorn had been climbed. But there had been an accident. They knew no more, and the Englishmen began to hasten down towards the village.

Meanwhile the Zermatt guides went on towards the Hohlicht slopes. They mounted higher and were soon able to look across to the whole height of the Matterhorn, its great north face deep in late afternoon shadow. And they saw, clustered near the foot of the slope, close up and under the lee of the rocks, what they could clearly identify as bodies. It was plain that they had fallen almost 4,000 feet. It was equally plain that they would be difficult to reach, so complex was the network of crevasses below them, and dangerous to remain by, so close did they lie under the cliffs. The men muttered a little glumly as they crossed themselves and turned back down the track to Zermatt.

Here, in the Monte Rosa, Robertson and his party heard the news from Seiler, and learned that Whymper was still asleep in his room. Shortly afterwards M'Cormick arrived. He had hurried down immediately on getting Whymper's note—and now realised, with a vividness which he was to recall until his death almost half a century later, how only his late arrival at Zermatt had kept him from the tragedy. Few of the Englishmen now present were much older than Whymper himself—M'Cormick was 30, Robertson 29, Yeats Browne 27.

The difficult ground below the North Face where the bodies were found

M'Cormick now went up to Whymper while the others waited below to see how best they could help. Then, later in the afternoon, the guides returned from the Hohlicht, and there arose the question of what was to be done next. There were, however, other things to be attended to. Seiler had of course immediately agreed to see that the families were informed. But it was clear, at least to M'Cormick and the others, that the death of four men on one mountain, in one accident, would raise protests, perhaps questions. The grand sport of mountaineering would suffer. Some statement, some almost semiofficial statement, should be issued. And surely Whymper should issue it. Whymper refused, as he was to do on more than one other occasion during the next fortnight—trying, as he later wrote to Robertson, to stick 'to the resolutions I made at Zermatt'. For, after all, whatever was said, however it appeared in the newspapers, it would inevitably bring the Taugwalders' name before the public eye. And for that Whymper had no taste whatever.

There was, moreover, the problem of deciding exactly what had really happened on the mountain. Was it Hadow who had slipped and pulled down the others, as seemed most likely? Could it have been Hudson? Could it even, unlikely as it seemed, could it even have been Croz? Was it, in fact, the surprise of such a thing that had drawn from old Peter those involuntary words: "What will Chamonix say?" These questions were not entirely answered by the account which Whymper gave to his friends—to M'Cormick first of all on the Saturday afternoon, and then later to Robertson, to Girdlestone and to the others. Indeed, they could not be entirely answered, and the reason for this was made clear in a letter to be written from Zermatt a few days later by the English chaplain at Geneva, sent post haste to the scene of the accident by the British Consul.

Meanwhile, there were the bodies to be brought back. Whymper had been dissuaded, only with difficulty, from following the party which had left Zermatt earlier and had returned with the news that there was no hope. Now he was eager that preparations should be pressed ahead for a start during the small hours of Sunday morning.

It is easy to understand the impasse that arose. Whymper had not seen the bodies with his own eyes. He was not the man to believe in miracles, but he believed in the vagaries of fate and it must have been difficult to rule out entirely the chance that someone of his four companions might still be alive. It was not, after all, so absurd. Men have rolled 2,500 feet and lived; it was always possible that some freak of fortune might have operated on the north face of the Matterhorn.

To the Zermatt men, all was different. They had seen the bodies. They knew there could he no survivors. Sunday was the traditional rest day. They proposed waiting until Sunday evening so that they would be able to reach the bodies at first light on Monday. As M'Cormick put it, they 'urged us, as there was no hope of saving any lives, to defer our expedition until they had made preparations for overcoming the difficulties of the way'. They also, no doubt, pointed out that in that case they would be able to attend Sunday mass before setting out. In the circumstances this seems natural enough. But in the communication from guides via Seiler to Whymper the story became garbled. Either that, or Whymper was unwilling to listen. Whatever the reason, one idea rooted itself in his head: that, as he was to put it, the guides of Zermatt, being 'threatened with excommunication by their priests if they did not attend the early Mass, were unable to accompany us'.

Now this was an ignorant observation, but it was one which many another man with Whymper's background might have made, even without the excuse of the circumstances, and it is hardly one for which he should be condemned. More surprising is the fact that he believed this in such company. Neither M'Cormick nor Robertson, neither Philpott nor Girdlestone can have believed the tale; all must have known that the words did not mean what they appeared to mean. Even the most bigoted churchman, let alone those now involved, knew the simple theological facts of life. That they failed to point these out to Whymper—or, more likely, failed to make him believe them—reveals, in either case, a lot about Edward Whymper. The result was, moreover, to have an unexpected effect on the picture of him that was to be painted for future generations. For this small grain of gritty, if explicable, criticism which his words cast on Catholics no doubt acted as the trigger which induced men such as Arnold Lunn to investigate just what sort of a man Whymper was at the time of the accident.

If the words were unfortunate, the situation was understandable. It is easy to imagine the growing acerbity, swelling to bitterness, as Whymper insisted that something must be organised at once, that preparations should already have been put in hand, that valuable time was being lost, that unless the Swiss did something, he would. And so on. With nerves strained and passions high, it would have been natural enough if the situation had boiled over into mutual recrimination.

As it was, Whymper got his way—and rightly so. If no one else would go, he would go alone. He knew the route as well as these local men, and he would put them to shame. If any of those present wished to come, he would be grateful, but if not he would manage as best he could.

Robertson agreed to come. So did M'Cormick. So did Philpotts. That made three clergymen and Whymper. There then arose the question of guides. Robertson and Philpotts readily agreed that Franz Andermatten should go with them. During the day Arthur Giles-Puller had come into the Monte Rosa with the Lochmatter brothers and he now willingly agreed that they should join the search party; Frederic Payot and Jean Tairraz from Chamonix, old friends of Croz, volunteered. Even so, the services of the five men were secured 'with some trouble', M'Cormick wrote. The Trade Union spirit among the guides, evidenced in what were still some grotesque restrictive practices, was strong. If the Zermatt men refused it would ill-become anyone else to blackleg.

Nevertheless the party was eventually made up. They set out at 2.00am on the Sunday with few words, the clatter of their boots alone breaking the silence of the village street. At first they took the route that Whymper had taken in such different circumstances less than three days previously—across the Zmuttbach and up the track to the Schwarzsee.

In the early light they plodded upwards over the ridge from the Hornli, then struck diagonally across to reach the Matterhorn Glacier. Even the Zermatt guides rarely came here, close up under the north face of the Matterhorn. Quite apart from the danger from rock falls, the glacier itself presented its own formidable difficulties—broken-up, badly crevassed, a maze of ice boulders, seracs, towers and pinnacles, as though an earthquake had rudely shaken a city of ice palaces and left the remains half-tottering to endanger all comers.

Here the party split into two, thus doubling the chance of finding a relatively easy route through the tangle. They ascended slowly through what was really the ice fall, carefully roped, cutting or enlarging steps as need be, occasionally retracing their route, always wondering whether some unexpected check might not cause them to turn back for a hundred yards or more.

It was nearly 8.30am when M'Cormick heard a shout from one of the guides in the group ahead. They had reached the top of the ice fall and were out on to the flatter portion of the glacier. A few minutes later his own party also reached the top and both hurried on towards the protruding rib of rock beyond which they knew the bodies must lie.

They reached the rocks. Neither Whymper nor, perhaps, even Robertson and the others had totally given up a lingering belief that some miracle might, after all, have taken place. That belief now vanished. 'As we saw one weatherbeaten man after another raise the telescope, turn deadly pale, and pass it on without a word to the next, we knew that all hope was gone,' wrote Whymper.

As the men moved towards the broken bodies they saw that they lay in the order in which they had descended. Croz was a little in advance, with Hadow near him and Hudson a little distance behind. Of Lord Francis Douglas there was no sign.

'All were naked and it was difficult to distinguish one from another,' Whymper later wrote to a friend. 'I could only identify Croz by his beard. Part of the lower jaw remained, but the upper part of the head had disappeared.'

It was indeed a grim sight. There was a smashed head, a forearm, a hand whose scars were recognised by Payot, an old friend of Michel Croz. There was a dismembered trunk and portions of a trouser with six gold coins still intact in the pocket, belonging to Croz. Lying beside him there were the smashed beads of his rosary. The crucifix was embedded in his jaw and this was dug out by Robertson with the aid of a penknife. Hudson was identified by his wallet and a letter from his wife that Whymper removed and put in his pocket. He gathered up also one of Hudson's gloves that lay on the snow, and the broad-brimmed English hat which he had given Croz only a short while previously.

As Whymper was moving about, there came a shout from the guides, a sudden crack from the rocks above, and then a shrapnel-fire of small stones. The guides and the Englishmen ran for cover under the lee of the rocks. All except Whymper, that is. Whymper disdained to notice the stones, moving without expression, his iron control still unbroken either by the macabre scene around him or by the fusillade from above.

He was looking at the rope, remnants of which were still attached to the bodies. And he now realised, apparently for the first time, that none of the three links between Croz and Hadow, Hadow and Hudson, Hudson and Lord Francis Douglas had been of the thinner line. The implication was now fully borne in upon him.

Meanwhile, the next move had to be made. The nine men began digging a communal grave. Eventually all was ready, and the shattered remains were moved into the shallow trench and covered first with a slab of ice and then with snow.

'Imagine us standing, with our bronze-faced guides, leaning on our axes or alpenstocks around that newly-made and singular grave, in the centre of a snowfield, perhaps never before trodden by man, with that awful mountain frowning above us, under a cloudless sky,' wrote M'Cormick.

He had retrieved Hudson's leather-bound prayer book, its brass hasp still shining and intact. He realised that it was the shorter version and turned therefore to Psalm 90: "Lord, thou hast been our refuge: from one generation to another. Before the mountains were brought forth..."

He continued through the whole seventeen verses as the men listened, the guides only half comprehending the English words, and with ears alert for sounds from above. M'Cormick repeated a number of prayers and part of the burial service.

Then, without a word, they picked up their axes and began their journey back to Zermatt.

Chapter ten

Enquiry

As the party approached Zermatt, Whymper may have felt that the whole terrible business was at last over. In fact, only one chapter was finished; another was about to begin.

Nearly 30 years later, when he described in a magazine that return to Zermatt on Sunday, July 16th, Whymper recalled one incident he had not previously mentioned. As the party neared the village, he says, they were met by old Peter Taugwalder. And old Peter, according to Whymper's testimony, went up to Robertson with the words, "Mr. Robertson, they say I cut the rope. Look at my fingers." And he splayed out his hands, for all to see where the rope had bitten into them.

Robertson was still alive when Whymper wrote this, and it seems unlikely that he invented the incident, which is of interest for two reasons. The fact that old Peter should go to Robertson rather than to Whymper gives a hint of the feeling that had already sprung up between the two men. And the fact that he should speak thus at all shows that even by that time, only 24 hours after the survivors had returned to the village, the ugly rumours were beginning to sprout.

The story of the cut rope is a stock-in-trade of the second rate novelist, dramatist and journalist. It had been drawn upon long before the Matterhorn accident, and it has survived even into present times when readers are better informed about what is possible upon the slopes of a mountain and what is not. It is convenient, simply explainable, dramatically satisfying, and in the overwhelming majority of occasions at variance with what could have happened. It was all these things in the case of the Matterhorn disaster. However, not everyone in Zermatt was interested in mountaineering. Quite a few of the inhabitants looked on the sport as a stupid nine-year wonder which brought a little money into the valley, but which interrupted the more homely seasonal round of activities. The use of rope to safeguard men when climbing steep rocks was a relatively recent innovation, and the mechanics of movement high on a mountain were probably unappreciated by most local folk. Yet they would know a little of such things; they would hesitate lightly to accuse one of their number of murder; and at least a few would have realised that even the most potentially murderous would have had no opportunity to 'cut the rope'.

But the legend had started, and it is not too difficult to see what may have set it upon its miserable way. When Whymper had closed up to old Peter after the accident he had, it will be remembered, been horrified to see the sash line. 'I made him give me the end,' he wrote. And it seems quite likely that under his instruction old Peter lopped off a foot or so of the thin rope with the knife he was to use for cutting lengths to safeguard the next part of the descent.

Back in Zermatt, Whymper would be strained beneath his outer calm; he would show to Robertson, to M'Cormick and the others, possibly to Seiler, the length of thin rope that had been cut off by old Peter. One can see how, even without the confusion of different languages, the transformation could have taken place as Whymper openly criticised the fact that the thinner rope had been used—this rope which had been the cause of the accident—this length which old Peter had cut off—had cut—this cause of the accident. From such a simple beginning it is possible to visualise the muddled facts spreading from Zermatt in ever widening circles. The process had already begun when Whymper and his companions returned to the village at about 2.00pm on that Sunday afternoon.

Girdlestone had by this time arrived back from Monte Rosa, having only heard of the accident late on the Saturday and having slept at the Riffel. He knew nothing of M'Cormick's arrival nor of Robertson and his party, and he immediately hurried down 'to comfort poor Whymper who had no other friend there.'

Now, as the British party told Seiler of the mountain burial,

Girdlestone came up to hear Whymper's account. Whymper told him the story that he was to repeat for the next 45 years. He gave more stress than he was later to give—possibly as a result of Girdlestone's questions—to the part that Hudson had played in the ascent. But he appears to have made no mention of the thinnest of the three ropes being used for the link between Douglas and old Peter, and he appears to have cast no slur on the Taugwalders. He had possibly been shocked by the absurd slanders on old Peter, and for the first time he no doubt began to realise how the story of the accident would gather fresh detail as it spread beyond the Valais into the outer world.

Yet he still refused to give a public account. It seems likely that more than one of the other Englishmen tried to make him change his mind that afternoon or evening.

Something would have to be said, it was stressed. There would, it was gently but firmly pointed out to him, be an official enquiry which would no doubt apportion blame if blame there were. He was no longer his own master. He owed it to the rest of the mountaineering community—more than one person may have added that he owed it to the Taugwalders—to give his account of events. Whymper still resisted the idea. But he at last agreed that something would have to be said. M'Cormick was, after all, the English chaplain in Zermatt. If anyone was to describe the accident, to give in to the clamour, then it should be M'Cormick.

The others agreed. So did M'Cormick who, in a letter to *The Times* dated Monday, July 17th, described how Hudson had left England with the intention of climbing the Matterhorn, having 'made a kind of ladder for scaling precipices'; how both he (M'Cormick) and Birkbeck had 'agreed to accompany him on his expedition' but had been prevented from doing so; and how Hudson and Hadow, Whymper and Douglas, had fortuitously formed one party which had made the successful ascent. He then came to the descent, and to the accident.

'Whymper was startled by an exclamation from Croz, and the next moment he saw Hadow and Croz flying downwards,' M'Cormick wrote.

'The weight of the two falling men jerked Hudson and Lord Francis Douglas from their feet. The two Taugvaulds [sic] and Whymper, having a warning of a second or two from the time that Croz called out, planted themselves as firmly as possible, to hold the others up. The pressure upon the rope was too much. It broke, and Croz, Hadow, Hudson and Lord Francis Douglas fell headlong down the slope and shot out of sight over a fearful precipice.' When he came to describe the action of the Zermatt guides the previous day, M'Cormick was restrained. They 'refused to go with us, as it would be Sunday, and urged us, as there was no hope of saving any lives, to defer our expedition until they had made preparations for overcoming the difficulties of the way,' he said.

M'Cormick's letter got the order on the rope right, although it was a day behind the incorrect message from the *Journal de Genève* correspondent. What it did not do, because it could not, was to underline exactly who slipped and under what circumstances. It still left a gap which most people were to feel could only be filled by a statement from Whymper.

Whymper did, in fact, make such a statement, probably that very day. But it was in effect a private one, written in the 'Livre des Etrangers' of the Monte Rosa. And, maddeningly in view of the circumstances, its wording is likely to remain forever unknown. For the account was subsequently ripped from the hotel book, for reasons which appear self-evident from the events which followed. For when Whymper returned to Zermatt in 1869 he wrote indignantly in the hotel book that his account had described the first ascent of the Matterhorn and of the accident. 'It bore testimony,' he went on, 'to the courage of those who so lamentably perished, to the devotion of Michel Croz and the gallantry of the guides Franz Andermatten and the brothers Lochmatter, who so nobly volunteered to seek the bodies of those who were lost, when not a single guide in Zermatt would move, in face of threatened excommunication by their priests.'

This note was in turn annotated, although by whom and when is not certain, since this page was also mutilated. It appears, however, that the addition was made by Bishop Mylne of Bombay who added the commonsense note: 'Owing to the brevity of the above statement one passage has been frequently misunderstood. As one of the nearest relatives of Mr. Hudson, I am anxious to state for the benefit of those who may hereafter read it that the threat of excommunication launched against the Zermatt guides was not intended to prohibit their taking part in the search, but to prevent their missing the Sunday morning mass (here the page is mutilated) . . . purpose. The fact that Michel Croz was a Roman Catholic should of course remove the idea that the object was to prevent their doing a service to those of another creed.'

It seems likely that Whymper wrote his note in Seiler's book on the night of Sunday, the 16th or on the following day. By this time, unknown to all in Zermatt, great events had been taking place on the other side of the frontier. They, too, like the long set of coincidences that had brought the members of the Hudson–Whymper party so tragically together, had an irony that could be seen only in later years, as the various pieces of the jigsaw were put together.

Whymper, describing his experiences on the summit, related how the Italians had 'turned and fled', and says how after a brief illusion of victory, the watchers at Breuil met the returning Italian party only to be told: "It is true. We saw them ourselves—they hurled stones at us! The old traditions are true—there are spirits on the top of the Matterhorn."

In fact, Jean-Antoine Carrel had immediately recognised Whymper by his light 'slop' trousers. And he knew, in that agonising moment, that he had let victory go by default. For by the time that Whymper had reached Zermatt with Lord Francis Douglas, Carrel had set up camp at nearly 13,000 feet. The weather was bad, but it would change; moreover, there was no one ahead of him on the Italian ridge and he was confident that no one would succeed from the Swiss side.

Thus on the night of July 13th Jean-Antoine Carrel and his party slept out on the Matterhorn at almost 13,000 feet while the British party rested on the Swiss side some 2,000 feet lower down.

The morning of the 14th broke as clear and confident for the Italians as it did for the British. But Carrel believed that he now had victory within his grasp and that no hurry was required. The party roused themselves in a leisurely way and left camp only at 6am. Twenty minutes later the British, who had been going for nearly three hours, had reached 12,800 feet. Thus the 'race for the summit', that common figment of the dramatist's imagination, did in fact develop on the slopes of the Matterhorn on the morning of the 14th. At least, it nearly developed. As with so many other episodes in the story of the Matterhorn, the evidence is contradictory. Yet it seems on balance that the Italians hardly raced, still feeling that victory was theirs for the taking.

Then, just before 2pm, while they were still some hundreds of feet below the summit, they saw the British party appearing, one by one, on the white crest of snow.

If only they had pressed on harder; if only they had realised that their ideas about the Swiss side might be wrong!

Little wonder that Carrel turned back in anger and shame and disgust. Many Italians were to say that he should have continued. Guido Rey, that great Italian mountaineer who was such a devotee of the Matterhorn, has explained in a few sympathetic phrases, why he retreated. 'He did not see what a fine *role* was still within his reach: namely, to proceed at all costs, to reach the summit a few hours after his rival, and, having solved the problem of the Italian ascent of the Matterhorn, to bring it as a gift to Giordano. It would have been a victory far more hardly won than the Englishman's! How came it to pass that Carrel did not see this was his duty?

'But no man can answer these questions, and perhaps Carrel himself could not answer, if he were alive. Only he who has been in places of great difficulty, a prey to doubts and fears, in face of the unknown, can know how under such circumstances a moral shock can paralyse in an instant all the energy that had been hoarded for years.'

Carrel turned back. He and his companions retreated to their camp, and on the Saturday, as Whymper was telling the story of the disaster in Zermatt, they descended to Breuil.

Here Carrel recovered himself. He would return. He would show that the Italian as well as the Swiss ridge could be climbed—if, that is, he could induce anyone to come with him. At first, all hung back. Then Aime Gorret, the 'beardless youth' who had made the first reconnaissance on the mountain with Carrel only eight brief years before, offered to accompany him. So did Jean-Baptiste Bich and Jean-Augustin Meynet, two men employed by Favre on the Jomein.

They left early on the Sunday morning and camped once more at the tent platform. On the Monday they left at dawn, quickly ascended to within 800 feet of the summit, and then found themselves entangled in some of the most difficult rock climbing they had so far faced.

Gorret was wounded on the arm by a falling stone. There was a clattering fall of icicles from above. Then, at the base of the final tower they reached an easier place which they named the Corridor. Even then, one more unexpected obstacle had to be overcome, for separating them from the summit there ran down a steep rock couloir. It was difficult to fix the rope that they saw would be needed for their return journey back across the couloir, so Gorret and Meynet remained on the nearer side while Carrel and Bich went on. They gained the ridge once more, clambered on and up, and soon after 3pm were on the summit, arriving there just about three days after the British party had left it. For Carrel it was a queer mixture of victory and defeat. He had reached the top. He had achieved victory from Breuil, he knew in his bones that many would follow him, and his peasant's sound financial instinct told him that he had put the makings of a good income into Favre's pocket. But he had not been the first.

The two Italians planted a flag by the cairn that the British had built. Down at the Jomein, Giordano had watched the good early morning weather cloud up, with much mist about the summit, as he wrote in his diary. 'Lifted a bit about 3.30,' he continued, 'and we saw our flag on the western summit of the Matterhorn. The English flag looked like a black shawl lying on the snow, in the centre.'

So the Matterhorn had at last been climbed from both south and north. Yet it was, paradoxically, over the northern and easier route that the sense of great difficulty was to remain the longer. Only a few could realise that while men had at last climbed the Italian ridge without disaster, the Swiss ridge, which had claimed four of its seven first successful assailants, was actually far less difficult.

All this lay in the future. On Monday, July 17th, Whymper realised that he would have to remain at Zermatt until the official enquiry had been held. M'Cormick, too, would remain, but Girdlestone, who had arranged to meet Hargreaves in Visp in the evening, set off down the valley that morning. The news that preceded him had not only come from the Randa correspondent of the *Journal de Genève*, for earlier that morning the Conseil d'Etat of the Canton of Valais wrote officially to Admiral Harris, Envoy-Extraordinary and Minister-Plenipotentiary and head of the British Legation in Berne.

The Valaisan authorities informed Harris that an accident had happened and that three Englishmen had been killed. There is one irony about this first official report since it said that the ascent had been made by four travellers, Lord Francis Douglas, the Rev. Charles Hudson and two others whose names were not known. The first official news of the Matterhorn disaster thus made no mention of Edward Whymper.

Admiral Harris immediately telegraphed the Consul in Geneva, Mr. Mackenzie, asking him for confirmation that Lord Francis Douglas had been killed. Confirmation—apparently gained from the *Journal de Genève*—came within a few hours, and on Tuesday Harris sent the following telegram to Lord Russell at the Foreign Office: 'Terrible accident at Zermatt Lord Francis Douglas Reverend Mr. Hudson Mr. Haddo [sic] Killed in descending Matterhorn Mr. Whymper survived the Reverend H Downton British Chaplain at Geneva has left for Zermatt relations sufferers should write him for details.'

Downton, a mild, conscientious man of 47 who had been serving in Geneva for eight years, had been alerted by Mackenzie immediately the latter had heard of the accident, and had started out for Zermatt at 6.00am on the Tuesday—without authority, a point which was to rumble down the archives for months. He took the train to Sion, then *voiture* to Visp where he arrived in time to hear that three of the bodies had been found.

Downton now travelled up the Vispthal on horseback, arriving later on Wednesday. The mail left early next morning, and Downton rose first thing to date, at 5.00am on the Thursday, his account of what he had learned.

'Sir,' he began,

'In passing through Sion on Tuesday, on my way here, I sent you a telegram containing all the information I could pick up there respecting the melancholy accident which took place on the Matterhorn on Friday last, the 14th inst.

'The facts mentioned in the telegram I find to have been substantially correct: except that as it might be inferred that all the bodies of those who perished had been found I afterwards ascertained that no trace of that of Lord Francis Douglas had been met with, but only his boots, empty, & which were identified by some peculiarity of make.

'The trousers of the guide, Michel Croz, were also found *empty* & but little torn. As I stated in the telegram, the respective bodies were recognised with difficulty. That of my dear friend, the Rev. Chas. Hudson, was distinguished only by a small part of one whisker which remained & a portion of the face & his clothes. A prayer book was found in his pocket. The body of Mr. Haddo was stripped nearly or quite of all clothing. An expedition, which started on Sunday morning, at 1am consisting of Mr. Whymper (the only survivor of the English who formed the party which had ascended the Matterhorn) Mr. Mc.Cormick, the Chaplain of Zermatt for this month, and two of the Masters of Rugby school, Messrs. Robertson and Phillips [sic] with five selected guides, having arrived with immense difficulty and danger at the spot, found the remains in the condition above described. It was a matter of extreme peril to remain on the spot as rocks & stones were falling continually, and as the guides could not be got to render any assistance, but lay down and *howled*, it was hastily resolved to cover up the mangled remains in the snow (the spot is one never visited by mortal) & the Chaplain read from Mr. Hudson's prayer book the 90th Psalm & repeated some portions of the burial service & the party returned. A sort of inquest has since been held in Zermatt by the *Syndic* of the *Canton*(?) and it has been ordered that the remains shall be brought down to Zermatt, where they are expected today, and where they will be interred in a meadow adjoining the Cemetery of the Village which surrounds the church. The guides sent officially on this service slept at 'the Chalets' last night to be ready for their duty today.

'The party descended the Matterhorn in the following order, which I give as, I think, a letter in the *Journal de Genève* gives it inaccurately. First Croz (the Chamonix guide), next Haddo, third Hudson, then Ld. F. Douglas fifth Taugwalder Senr., a Zermatt guide, sixth Mr. Whymper, last Taugwalder Jnr. The two last had remained a little longer on the summit but had joined the party & were connected with them by a rope when the accident occurred. Whymper says it impossible for the survivors to say, or conjecture, with any certainty which of the party slipped, as they were round a corner of rock & out of sight, only Croz the most advanced being visible. It is supposed to have been Haddo as the least experienced but the Chaplain, Mr. Mc.Cormick, himself much accustomed to mountaineering, tells me that the most experienced might have slipped at the particular spot, where there was only a small footing of rock, and that slanting.

'The Master of this Hotel, M. Seiler, told me last night that a boy of the village with a small telescope had seen two or three persons on the mountain about 3 o'clock. That half an hour afterwards he had observed what he described as an avalanche. M. Seiler had said that that was impossible as there was no snow to form one. He has no doubt since that what he saw was the party who fell, who rolling over & over, habited chiefly in white and light coloured clothing, might give the boy this idea! They fell some 4,000 feet.

'I have no time at present for any further details, but have to add the melancholy fact that on the evening of Tuesday the 18th another fatal accident occurred in the neighbourhood of the Riffelhorn to Mr. Wilson, a Master at Rugby, Fellow of Clare College, Cambridge, who had left his companions towards the evening to bathe in the lake of the Riffelberg &

is supposed afterwards to have ascended the Riffelhorn, or part of it. His body was brought down last evening to Zermatt & now awaits internment in a Chalet near this Hotel!

'The post is now starting. I have written in great haste at the request of M. Mackenzie, the Consul at Geneva. I have the Honour to be, Sir,

Your very obed^{nt}. Servant, Henry Downton,

English Chaplain at Geneva.'

This letter, which gives a different, and possibly more embroidered account of the finding of the bodies, is of interest for one particular reason. First M'Cormick then Girdlestone, and then Yeats Browne heard from Whymper his account of the accident. All of them agree that there is some supposition about who it was who really slipped; yet all of them infer that even though there is doubt about it being Hadow, there is not much doubt. Downton's letter, written by a man who had come to gather an account of the accident that was at least semi official, stresses that none of the survivors had in fact been able to see the leading figures at the crucial moment. It is possible, of course, that Downton interpreted the same set of statements differently from the others; nevertheless it seems possible that in the earlier cases Whymper was loosely recounting events to another mountaineer. With Downton, he was speaking to a man more than 20 years his senior, despatched by the British Consul; he may well have found it more fitting to cross the 'T's', dot the 'I's', and underline the fact that no one really knew exactly how the accident occurred.

By the Thursday morning something else was astir. For the Syndic of the Commune, as Downton had reported, had now met and agreed that it was wrong for the bodies to be left where they were. Proper burial was demanded, and late on the afternoon of Wednesday the 19th a convoy of nineteen guides set out from Zermatt for the last chalets on the path to the Matterhorn Glacier. Here they spent Wednesday night, setting out from their improvised resting place at first light the following morning. It had been hoped that an early start would minimise the dangers of the operation, since the men should be clear of the more dangerous spots before the sun began to free stones from the upper slopes. This was the case. But the party which brought the shattered bodies into Zermatt on Thursday morning reported how narrowly they had escaped disaster; for a giant serac had toppled and shattered itself into fragments across their path only a few moments after they had passed. The bodies were put in plain coffins and laid in a room near the Roman Catholic church which had been specially prepared by the Seilers. The funeral took place on Friday—or rather funerals, for Croz was buried first, and the British an hour later.

Robertson and Philpott were by this time up at the Riffel and at the funeral in the little churchyard the only English present were Whymper, M'Cormick and Yeats Browne, the latter deeply impressed by Whymper, that 'strong hard man' as he described him. Whymper had showed him the broken end of the rope as he had described the accident. 'He also put into my hands the top of the Matterhorn,' Yeats Browne later wrote, 'a bit of syenite, one half the size of a cricket ball, which I handled with semi-superstitious veneration.'

The funeral was only the first of Whymper's trials on Friday, July 21st. He 'suffers awful mental anguish', the Rev. W. Prior wrote to Mackenzie in Geneva. 'The poor fellow will go beside himself if he does not leave the place.' He had, however, been unable to leave until the authorities had set up their court of Enquiry and heard his evidence. Its members were now ready.

Their task was to elucidate the facts, to issue a judgment which might or might not report negligence, apportion blame, and suggest what further steps, if any, should be taken. It was fitting that they should therefore meet on neutral ground, as remote as possible both from the people of the village, two of whose guides were involved, and from the Englishman. They were to hear evidence in private, as was the custom of the country, and they required a room where they could be decently shuttered away from the rest of the village, where they could hear the facts in peace, and with a judicial calm that none of them may have felt. It might have seemed almost improper to meet at the Monte Rosa, so steeped had its very bricks become in the conquest of the mountains surrounding the head of the valley. They thus chose the new Hotel du Mont Cervin, a few hundred yards down the road from the Monte Rosa and on the other side of the village street.

Here there came on the 21st the examining magistrate, Joseph Antoine Clemenz, who had travelled up the 20-mile track from Visp, the last village or small town which lay where the Vispthal debouched into the Rhone Valley. With him was the deputy recorder, Cesar Clemenz; the clerk of the court Donat Andenmatten; and the huissier or bailiff, especially impressed for the occasion, Jean Julen. All were sound, solid men, innocent it appears of any specialist knowledge of mountaineering, shocked no doubt by events, ready to do whatever unpleasant duty lay before them but perhaps a little unconfident of themselves, uncertain of what questions should be asked; four men suddenly transported from the worthy and humble round of local death and minor disaster to a task upon which the bright glare of international publicity might well have been cast. Luckily perhaps for those most closely involved, no glare came. A century and a half ago, 'news interest' gathered impetus more slowly. The simple facts of the Matterhorn accident were only just sinking in. The reaction was to come only later, and on July 21st few of those in the outside world knew much about events at the head of an obscure Alpine valley in a small village which was difficult to reach and could be found only with trouble on some of the maps.

The first witness to be called to the room in the Hotel du Mont Cervin was Edward Whymper. As an Englishman he was not used to being summoned to give evidence before foreigners. But even Edward Whymper must have felt more than a tremor as he stood before the four men and the enquiry opened.

"Your name, age, profession, residence?"

The first formalities were soon over, and he was taken question by question through the course of the vital few days. He had been a member of the expedition which had left on the 13th to climb the Matterhorn? How many were in the expedition? What were their names? At what time did they leave their bivouac for their summit on the morning of the 14th? At what time did they arrive, and how long did they stay?

Whymper replied calmly and without hesitation, describing the simple facts. Then came question No. 10 referring to the descent.

"Were the four tourists and the guides tied together by ropes?" Whymper replied that they were, gave the order of descent, and added: "Between Lord Douglas and the elder Taugwalder the rope was thinner than that between Michel Croz and Lord Douglas on one side and the elder Taugwalder and Taugwalder junior on the other."

Curiously, perhaps, no member of the court asked for any explanation of this somewhat surprising statement—an omission that may have been due either to an unwillingness to ask embarrassing questions, or to an ignorance of just how important the matter was.

Whymper then described how the accident had occurred. The two vital sentences—translated from the French version, since no record exists of Whymper's words—were: "I cannot say with certainty what was the true cause of the accident. But I believe that Michel Croz had placed Hadow's feet on their holds ('sur des points de rochers') and was about to turn to make a step himself when Hadow slipped and in his fall knocked over Michel Croz." Whymper never actually altered this story, but throughout the years one senses a slight change of emphasis. The "cannot say with certainty" is usually retained in one form or another but it no longer has such prominence and, as time goes on, one gathers increasingly the impression that any doubt about who did in fact slip is more technical than real. This is natural enough. As Whymper told the story, in various editions of the *Scrambles*, in newspaper articles and on lecture platforms, the doubts would naturally begin to fade away. On July 21st they were still almost as strong as they had been two days previously when he spoke to Downton.

Whymper described the finding of the bodies, and was then brought up by being asked: "Have you not reported to the Zermatt authorities that you have found the bodies of three of the victims?"

"Not officially," Whymper was forced to admit. But he had told the

President of the Commune of the accident on the Saturday morning, and as a result men had gone out to look for them. "The same Zermatt guides" he added—and one can imagine with what bitterness he pronounced the words—"the same Zermatt guides refused in a body to bring back the bodies the following Sunday, and it was for that reason that I went out, without official authority, to bring back the bodies, and that on my return I believed that I was not able to make an official report."

He explained that the only traces found of Lord Francis Douglas had been a pair of gloves and the leather belt which he had worn during the ascent, and he was asked if there was anything he wished to change in his account, or anything which he wished to add. There was one small point. "From our departure on the morning of the 14th the younger Taugwalder who to begin with had accompanied us as a porter, now served as guide."

There had been seventeen questions in all. None of them had dealt with the really vital matters—who was in charge, who planned the order of descent, why the weaker rope was used.

Old Peter was called next. Aged 45, married, mountain guide, domiciled in Zermatt.

One can imagine him giving the answers with an implied wonder that men should have to ask such obvious questions; almost certainly dressed in his Sunday best; probably cursing inwardly the ill fortune that had treated him of all people thus—the man who knew the Matterhorn better than them all.

He had been engaged by Lord Francis Douglas and Whymper. And had he, the enquiry asked, coming slowly nearer to the knuckle, been told of those who were to make the attempt; had he commented—either on those who were to take part or against the disproportionate number of tourists and guides?

"They told me," he replied, "how many people were going. I didn't comment on any particular person. However, I remarked that, considering the number of tourists, there were too few guides. Whymper and Hudson replied that they went"—'marchaient' as it is given, a key word which might have meant 'went', 'walked', or in the context even 'climbed'—"as well as guides, after which I made no further comment."

Taugwalder was then questioned as to how, and by whom, the leading members of the party were roped up on the summit. Having described how the first four members had been tied he explained that he himself had tied on to Lord Francis Douglas.

"Why," he was asked, "did you use another rope?" "Because," came the perfectly reasonable answer, "the first rope wasn't long enough for me to tie on to."

"This rope used between Lord Douglas and yourself—was it, as you suggest ('*suivant vous*') stout enough?"

Here, if the enquiry had been held in public, there would certainly have come one of those little silences. One has heard them in murder cases and in War Crimes trials, even in humble situations where a man is accused of a simple unpremeditated killing by driving a motor car when his mind was befuddled. They come, one cannot help feeling, because some instinct tells both the specialist and the ordinary man that all drives towards one watershed of a question, just as it drives men to one resolving situation on a mountain.

What had old Taugwalder really thought about that rope? The answer, of course, is that he had thought nothing at all. It was, after all, the rope which Whymper himself was later to describe as 'of a kind that I used formerly'.

"If I had found that the rope used between Lord Douglas and myself was not strong enough I would have taken care not to link myself with it to Lord Douglas, and I would not have wished to put him in danger any more than myself (` ... je me serail bien gardé de m'attacher avec elle à Lord Douglas et je n'aurais pas voulu le mettre en danger, pas plus que moimême'). If I had found this rope too weak, I would have recognised it as such before the ascent of the Matterhorn and I would have turned it down."

There it was. The words ring as true today as they did in the room of the Mont Cervin a century and a half ago. The four men holding the enquiry felt the truth coming out, and it is a pity that they did not subsequently make this known.

Then old Peter was brought to exactly what had happened. His version was different in one important detail from the account that Whymper had given a short while previously. They had reached, as he described it, a place where there were only polished slabs and where it was very difficult to get a good foothold. "It was here that the first tourist following the guide Croz slipped and dragged off those behind him, and they in turn all involved the guide Croz after the rope between Lord Douglas and myself had broken."

Croz had not been sent flying by Hadow, who had slipped past him and dragged off first Hudson and then Lord Francis Douglas, and there had then come a moment when Croz, alone, held three men on a single rope before being dragged to destruction. That was old Peter's version.

Had all precautions been taken? Taugwalder was asked. They had. "However," he added, "it is regrettable that the first man after Croz was a very bad climber."

And how, persisted the enquiry, had the accident happened—trying no doubt to force out the fact of Hadow's kick into Croz's back, a fact that had not even been mentioned by Taugwalder.

"I've already described it," Taugwalder said, according to the report of the Enquiry. This answer tends to reinforce the belief that the official record was one which, while perfectly honest, may well have been tailored together from verbatim statements, reported question and answer, which lost precision in translation.

There was, at least, a little simplicity about the questions, for after Taugwalder had described how he and his son and Whymper had descended to Zermatt he was asked whether "at the moment of the fall of the tourists the rope had or had not been taut?" He replied that it had been, but neither the question nor the answer gives any indication of which rope was meant—that between Taugwalder and Douglas, Douglas and Hudson, Hudson and Hadow or between Hadow and Croz.

Taugwalder was then asked to give his opinion about the breaking of the rope. "I am not able to say, but the weight of three men with the force of their fall would have broken a really strong rope." He explained that it was impossible, once the rope had broken, to do anything about the four falling men. And he faced what in other company would have been regarded as the 64,000-dollar question.

"If the rope between you and Douglas had not broken, would you have been able to save the tourists?"

If the answer was "No", it could be inferred that only the breaking of the rope had saved the lives of the Taugwalders and Whymper. If the answer was "Yes", it cast into deeper shadow his decision to use the weaker rope for that one link.

Yet old Peter went even farther than a straight "Yes" or "No" reply. "I have the steady conviction," he replied, "that if the rope had not broken between Lord Douglas and myself I would have been able, with the aid of the guide Croz, to save the tourists."

Once again, that assumption that Croz was still standing firm after the breaking of the rope. And, more important, once again an answer which suggests that Taugwalder, like the rest, may well have been muddled on the summit, befuddled by victory, and that his choice of rope depended on chance rather than on a cool calculating estimate of possible disaster.

Old Peter's answer was his last for the day. He was followed by Franz Andenmatten who merely gave evidence that he had first found the bodies of three of the victims on the Sunday morning and had subsequently gone up with the larger party of Zermatt guides to bring them down for burial.

Andenmatten's evidence ended the day's proceedings. There seemed little more to be said or done, but on the Saturday the Court met again and Alexander Lochmatter gave evidence that he, also, had taken part in the Sunday morning search and had helped to bury the three bodies. Neither Andenmatten nor Lochmatter were, of course, questioned about the accident and the Court appears to have concerned itself, naturally enough, with the fact that the body of Lord Francis Douglas had not been found, and that the bodies of the three victims had at first been buried, in effect, 'irregularly'.

That appeared to be all. The Court had done its task as well as could be expected. Its members had, it is true, asked none of the vital questions, nuzzled down to none of the unresolved problems. Yet it is both charitable and reasonable to assume that they failed not through any wish to cover up the Taugwalders but because the matter was beyond their compass. They had elucidated, as far as was possible, what had happened. The unresolved consisted of answers to the question 'why'—why had there been no firm leadership on the mountain? Why had the order of descent been so casual? Why, above all, had the choice of ropes been what it was? All these were things which depended on the inter-relationship of various forces in men's minds. They would provide—have, in fact, provided—material for dissection and argument by the experts, for learned theses, for prognostications and speculations. They were beyond the range of simple men trying to discover merely who tied on to whom, and which rope broke—and, quite possibly as important in their eyes, why one body was missing and three others had been buried irregularly.

Yet the work of the Court was not yet finished. It was to meet once more, on the Sunday, to recall old Peter, and to put to him a set of questions which were based on suggestions by Whymper. Whymper himself, describing the finding of the bodies on the Matterhorn Glacier, and noting that only the Douglas-Taugwalder link had been of the thinner rope, later wrote: 'For the sake of the old guide (who bore a good reputation), and upon all other accounts, it was desirable that this matter should be cleared up; and after my examination before the Court of Enquiry which was instituted by the Government was over, I handed in a number of questions which were framed so as to afford old Peter an opportunity of exculpating the grave suspicions which at once fell upon him.'

It is not at all clear when Whymper decided that this was necessary. However, on the Saturday the Court sat only to hear Lochmatter, of whom they asked ten questions, and it is reasonable to suppose that when they rose no further work was in view. The Court sat in private. But it is difficult not to believe that old Peter will have recounted the questions he was asked. It is difficult not to believe that Whymper, and the other Englishmen at the Monte Rosa, will have discussed what had been asked and what replied, what conclusions might be drawn from it all. Thus it was probably some time on Saturday that Whymper decided that further questions should be put to old Peter.

No copy of Whymper's original questions appears to have survived, and the translated Minutes were made available by the Swiss authorities only after Whymper's death. It is, therefore, impossible to know whether the note which he presumably handed over to M. Clemenz did suggest, as one might expect it to suggest, that old Peter should be asked why the rope was chosen on the summit. When the guide was recalled on Sunday the questions, once again, avoided this nub of the matter.

First, he was asked whether his recollection of the accident had changed since he had previously given evidence; had he anything to add or to change? Only, he replied, that before they arrived at the dangerous stretch he had mentioned to Croz that they might fix a rope. But Croz had replied that this wasn't necessary.

Did his son know how the accident had happened? Old Peter thought not, since he had shouted out at the time, "Are you still there, father?"

The Court then returned to the order on the rope, and the fact that there were three amateurs behind Croz, a fact adequately explained by Hudson's insistence that he could be counted on to do the job of a guide.

For a moment the Court skirted round the essential point, asking who had provided the rope which linked old Peter and Lord Francis Douglas. The answer was simple—the tourists.

There followed a question about whether young Peter was really porter or guide. Then, rather inconsequentially, a question about the time that they had left Zermatt on the 13th, the time that they had arrived at their tent site and the time that they had left it the following morning.

Only then did the Court come to a matter of genuine importance. It did not question the choice of rope on the summit. But it did try to resolve the two differing versions of the accident given by Whymper and

Taugwalder. Whymper, M. Clemenz pointed out, had stated that Hadow had knocked over Croz and that they had pulled off Hudson and Lord Francis Douglas in turn. Old Peter had omitted any reference to Croz having been knocked over, and had said that he had been involved only after the rope had broken—implying that only the weight of three falling men had dragged him from his steps.

"In view of the fact that Mr. Whymper's evidence and your own do not entirely conform," M. Clemenz asked, "do you stand by your earlier reply?"

Here old Peter was in a treble difficulty. None of the survivors could fairly claim to be certain of what had happened. They were strung out in a difficult and dangerous situation. They were watching their own steps, the rope immediately in front. Secondly, after even a short interval, could one, in any case, really be sure? Thirdly, and perhaps almost as important, could one really flatly contradict one's masters?

"Since Mr. Whymper was above me, and in a position from which he was able to see what was going on ('d'ou it pouvait se rendre compte de ce malherueux accident'), his evidence could be more precise, so that I do not wish to maintain that Croz must have fallen after the three other tourists. Everything happened in a flash, and we were so surprised that it is, so to speak, impossible to say exactly what happened."

Taugwalder was asked, once again, if he had anything to add or to alter.

He added only that as the rope between Whymper and himself was not tight he was able to turn to the rocks and take a turn of it over a rock projection, and that this enabled him to save himself. "The rope which attached me to Douglas and the others gave me such a shock with the fall that I am still suffering where it passed round my body," he commented.

On that note the enquiry ended.

Of those who had been involved in the first ascent of the Matterhorn, three were buried, one still lay on the crags of the mountain. Young Peter Taugwalder was already in another part of the Alps, working with fresh employers to whom he gave every satisfaction. Old Peter remained in Zermatt protesting, as we shall see, at the manner in which he had been treated by Whymper, who was himself now told that he could leave the village. Girdlestone was by this time in the Oberland, preparing to attempt the Jungfrau, while Downton had departed down the road to Visp, probably thankful that the wretched business was over. At least, he thought it was over. In fact, the repercussions of his journey to Zermatt were to reverberate through the Foreign Office files for months—the cause being a matter of 250 francs, or roughly £9.4.0d.

For Mackenzie in Geneva had not sought authority before sending his colleague to Zermatt, believing, as he wrote to the Foreign Office, that 'in a contingency like the present . . . the public naturally expect Her Majesty's Consuls to be the first to act'. This slip of the routine made it, however, almost impossible for Downton's expenses to be paid from public funds. The argument dragged on, with protest and counter-protest passing between Geneva, Berne and Whitehall. On November 25th, four months later, Mackenzie informed London that £5 had now come in privately from the Marquess of Queensberry; but what about the remaining £4.4? A few days later the matter was finally settled. Mr. Hadow, Douglas Hadow's father, had also heard of the matter and had provided the outstanding amount. Mackenzie could now conclude by 'apologising for having troubled your Lordship at all on the subject'.

CHAPTER ELEVEN

WHAT THE CRITICS SAID

WHYMPER WAS FREE TO LEAVE ZERMATT once he had given his evidence, and he in fact left on Saturday, before the men holding the Enquiry had completed their hearings.

But first he had to settle accounts with the Taugwalders. Young Peter had left the village soon after the accident, while old Peter appears to have kept out of Whymper's way, possibly to avoid any accusation of collusion in the evidence which they were to give before the Enquiry. Now Whymper handed over to old Peter a total of 235 francs that included 100 for himself for the ascent of the Matterhorn, 80 for young Peter, and 20 for Joseph's ascent as far as the tent platform; in addition there was 15 francs for Joseph's trip across the Théodule with Lord Francis Douglas and a collective bonne main of 20 francs—the equivalent of about £9 in all which Whymper subsequently described as 'the highest price ever given for mountain ascents'.

Now the Enquiry was over. The last rites had been performed. Accounts had been settled. As Whymper strode down the Vispthal to Visp, where he arrived late at night, he must have felt that the whole unhappy business was at last finished. He was soon to be disillusioned.

From Visp he crossed the Gemmi Pass to Kandersteg and on the following day, Monday the 24th, reached Interlaaken. And in Interlaaken, possibly in the public reading room, he realised what a stir the Matterhorn accident had created in Europe. The news had been treated sensationally, as was perhaps justified by events, and inaccurately as was perhaps inevitable in the circumstances. Four men killed on one mountain, and one of them an English milord; a broken rope; a party of another nationality on the far side of the mountain—all these were not merely the stuff of popular journalism. They were something more. The more shabby inaccuracies and distortions might be soon forgotten or corrected. Yet the story of the ascent of the Matterhorn continued to represent a laboratory specimen of man's growing domination of the natural world— that feature of the century in which the inhabitants of Europe in general, and of Britain in particular, took such pride. Man staking out ever farther the bounds of his empire and man paying his price—this was the theme that remained when the personal drama of the climb had been dealt with and after the morals of mountaineering for pleasure had been fully debated.

At least a little of this appears to have been appreciated at last by Edward Whymper. He was no more anxious than before to explain to uninformed readers what had happened on the mountain; he still despised the common touch. Yet he realised that some explanation was owed to the mountaineering fraternity, and that a wider public would demand its pound of explanation. He therefore wrote two letters. The first was sent to E. von Fellenberg of the Swiss Alpine Club, with French and German translations, and with the suggestion that it might be passed on to the *Journal de Genève* and *Der Buna*. The second letter, in similar terms, was sent to Signor Rimini, the Hon. Secretary of the Italian Alpine Club. In both Whymper told the story which he was to repeat throughout life, a story whose broad lines have never seriously been in doubt.

Before leaving Interlaaken for London Whymper also wrote to M'Cormick, asking how best he could claim back from the Valais authorities the expenses of what he called his 'detention' at Zermatt, since he was 'not pleased at having been detained there so long, merely, as it seems to me, to suit M. Clemenz' pleasure'. He then crossed the Channel and travelled down from London to Town House, Haslemere, the home into which his family had moved with Joseph Whymper's second wife some six years previously.

The sight of the Continental papers had alerted him for criticism. Yet it is unlikely that he was prepared for the onslaught of *The Times* which met him with his first breakfast on English soil for more than a month.

What was published on July 27th was not merely a *Times* leader; it was a first leader, giving the Matterhorn, and the issues it raised, equal place with the rise and fall of empires, the state of the nation, and the grave issues of political and moral conduct on to which the leader-writers of the Thunderer normally trained their heaviest guns. This 1,600 word commentary on the accident did not decry danger or the taking of chances; but it demanded that the rewards should be fitting, seemly, and easily understood by the mass of *The Times* readers if not by the mass of mankind. 'What is the use of scaling precipitous rocks, and being for half an hour at the top of the terrestrial globe?' it asked. 'There is use in the feats of sailors, of steeple climbers, vane cleaners, chimney sweeps, lovers and other adventurous professions. A man may be content to die in such a cause, for it is his life's battle. But in the few short moments a member of the Alpine Club has to survey his life when he finds himself slipping, he has but a sorry account to give of himself. What is he doing there, and what right has he to throw away the gift of life and ten thousand golden opportunities in an emulation which he only shares with skylarks, apes, cats, and squirrels?' The Alpine Club, 'that has proclaimed this crusade', must manage things better, it was added, and there was then suggested a series of admonitions about practice, training and caution almost fitting for a 20th century open air movement, concluding with an injunction to the Club that 'above all things, their ropes must not break'. However, in spite of this admission that men might insist on climbing anyway, the nub of the leader was summed up in its questions—'But is it life? Is it duty? Is it common sense? Is it allowable? Is it not wrong?'

Considering the climate of the period, and the information on which *The Times* had to form its opinions, it was a leading article somewhat less unreasonable than has often been claimed. For the information was still extremely scanty. Even the Queen showed some confusion, writing in her diary a few days earlier that: 'Four poor Englishmen, including a brother of Lord Queensberry, have lost their lives in Switzerland, descending a very dangerous place from the Matterhorn, and falling over a precipice.' There was still uncertainty about the details of the tragedy. And here one returns, as did many of those involved, to the figure of Edward Whymper, the only British survivor; the only one, indeed, who might be expected to give a coherent account and put the tragedy into perspective—if perspective there were.

The leading article in *The Times* called for a quick rejoinder from Whymper. It was ten days before he made it, and during those ten days events moved on in both Switzerland and England.

In Switzerland the Valais authorities had taken note of the report submitted to them by M. Clemenz, and of the conclusions which he and his colleagues had reached. But they preserved a clam-like silence, a silence which was to be preserved for more than half a century, was to help keep alive the feeling that some major mystery might lie concealed, and was also to leave the elder Taugwalder in the position of a man accused by rumour and unable to clear himself. To Admiral Harris in Berne, the President of the Valais sent a brief resume of what Whymper had said at the enquiry, and the statement that old Peter had agreed with Whymper's evidence.

The British Mission in Berne was to be further involved, for a few days later a cousin of Lord Francis Douglas asked the authorities for a copy of the evidence which Whymper had given at the enquiry—apparently preferring this, for reasons which they thought sufficient, to writing to Whymper direct. He was duly provided with the information a few days later.

Admiral Harris's staff was also asked to trace the whereabouts of Lord Queensberry himself. News of the accident had reached the Queensberry home in Glen Stuart on Wednesday the 19th, as preparations were being completed for the young Marquess's coming-of-age the following day. All preparations were cancelled, and within hours John Sholto Douglas, the 8th Marquess was on his way to Zermatt. His impetuousness is reflected both by the local comment—'it is to be hoped that he will not expose himself to needless danger in an effort to recover the remains of his unfortunate brother'—and by the memory of him that remained weeks afterwards in Zermatt. 'He would stay in the same room and bed his brother had occupied and . . . one morning he started off, leaving a letter on the table saying he was going to look for his brother. He was alone and without any provisions. They followed and found him near the foot of the mountain, half crazy.'

The failure to discover the missing body was now to bring on to the scene the one Englishman who, with the sole exception of Whymper, had made the most determined assaults on the Matterhorn.

This was Professor Tyndall who, early in July had travelled to the eastern Oberland with his young friend Thomas Hirst. They intended climbing the Todi, experienced trouble with their guides, and began a leisurely tour westwards. On the evening of Tuesday the 18th Tyndall and Hirst arrived late at Gadmen and went to their rooms without hearing the news which had by this time spread eastwards through Switzerland. As they were about to leave the inn the following morning, the Professor was asked by a local guide whether he knew Douglas. "He is killed, sir," the man continued, "killed upon the Matterhorn."

It became evident that some disaster had occurred, but only the following day did Tyndall and his companion hear the real story. They continued westwards, through Kandersteg and then over the Gemmi Pass and down to Visp where they arrived on the 30th. Here, in the little town which had provided M. Clemenz for the Enquiry, they gathered more details; at St. Niklaus, which they reached later that day, Tyndall probably heard that the elder brother had been contemplating desperate efforts to find the missing body.

It is not clear how much of this was known in St. Niklaus by the night of the 30th when Tyndall and Hirst arrived. But judging by Tyndall's manuscript journal he was, when he walked up the track to Zermatt the following morning, already considering a daring plan to search for the missing body; and in a letter to Faraday he explained that he 'had been informed that Lord Francis Douglas' mother suffered much from the idea of her son not having been found'.

As Tyndall and Hirst passed a group of road makers Tyndall noted with his usual careful observation that the men making cavities in the rocks for the blasting charges could drive a hole a foot deep in hard granite in less than an hour. 'I immediately resolved to pick out from those men a competent climber, take him with me to the point at which the party slipped, drive irons into the rocks there and descend the precipices by means of ropes attached to the irons,' he wrote in his journal.

This was an audacious idea, conceivable only by a man with Tyndall's unusual combination of mountaineering ability and scientific acumen; it was also an extremely unpopular one. 'The Zermatt guides would have nothing to do with the project—the accident seemed to have paralysed them,' Tyndall wrote. Nevertheless he managed to conscript the younger Lochmatter who had appeared before the Court of Enquiry, and at Zermatt Tyndall and Lochmatter prepared their plans. First of all, orders were given for the assembly of numerous 'boring irons'. Then came the question of rope. Tyndall estimated that 3,000 feet of first quality stuff would be needed. Lochmatter was therefore despatched to Geneva, whence he returned four days later, bringing up the load—almost 200 lbs of it—on heavily laden mules. By the time that it arrived, the hammers, steel punches, iron bars, and a tent were all ready, and these were moved up to the Schwarzsee chapel. By this time Tyndall's ambitious plans appear to have become even more ambitious. 'I proposed,' he wrote in his journal, 'driving in bars at the more difficult places, stretching a rope from bar to bar, thus forming a balustrade which would render the descent of those difficult places speedy [and] secure.'

It is fascinating to speculate on what the outcome would have been had he, Lochmatter, and the few other venturesome men drawn into the enterprise, finally embarked on this impressive expedition. But the weather had broken. With the turn of the month the conditions which had allowed first the British party and then the Italians to reach the summit, had suddenly changed. Day followed day during which the upper slopes were wreathed in clouds; when they occasionally cleared it was seen that fresh snow covered the mountain—snow which thawed, froze, re-thawed, and froze again, coating the rocks with a slippery layer and transforming even the easiest passages into places where one could easily slip and slide to destruction.

On at least two occasions the weather began to clear, and Tyndall warned Lochmatter to be ready the following morning; but each time the clouds had closed in once again. Then Tyndall himself took a bad fall on the path down from the Riffelhorn. Time was running out. He was due at Geneva for a scientific meeting within a few days. And eventually he was forced to leave Zermatt, taking the track down to St. Niklaus, ice axe in hand and with a huge coil of rope over his shoulder. 'He told me,' says Newman Hall, the Congregationalist divine who met him on the track, 'that the mother of Lord Douglas had a morbid idea that her son was still alive on the rocks. He knew this to be impossible.'

Almost exactly three years later Tyndall himself was to make the first traverse of the Matterhorn, climbing the mountain from Breuil, passing over the summit and then descending what was roughly the route the first party had taken. When he saw the crags at close quarters, he began to think that his scheme for recovering the body would have had little chance of success; most of the Zermatt people thought so from the start, and the only other serious proposals came from Melchior Moor, a guide of Gadmen who wrote to the British authorities in Berne offering to search for the body. There is no evidence that he was encouraged. 'I should be inclined only to reward the searchers in the event of the body being found,' Admiral Harris wrote to one of the Douglas relatives, 'and it is a question whether holding out this would not be exposing men to fruitless risk of their lives.'

The failure to find the missing body left one loose end of the unhappy story flapping in the breeze of rumour. The failure of the Enquiry to make public the evidence which it had heard provided another. So, one can well imagine, did the dark stories which continued to spread. These did not concern only culpability about the choice of ropes. The belief that a monetary reward had been offered, by persons unspecified, to anyone making the first ascent of the Matterhorn, was 'universal' according to Charles Parker who arrived in the village on July 29th.

It was Parker who with his two younger brothers had made the first of all amateur explorations of the Matterhorn five years previously, and to him Taugwalder now claimed that he had been promised much more money than he had been paid. 'I thought,' wrote Parker to his father, 'I could hardly refuse his request to make some enquiry for him in England.' It is perhaps a significant statement, coming as it did from a man such as Parker, then private secretary to the Secretary of State for War and soon to become M.P. and Privy Councillor.

By the first week of August there was thus a good deal of uncertainty, suspicion, and ill will hanging in the Valais air, and some feeling, supported by nothing more substantial than rumour, that someone was concealing something. Much the same might be said of the situation in England.

The Times leader had released what was now seen to be a deep public concern about the sport of mountaineering. John Cowell, a former Secretary of the Alpine Club, had immediately written to *The Times* pointing out that the Club led no 'crusade', had done much to encourage such worthy operations as the mapping of the Alps, and could proudly claim that since its foundation eight years before none of its members had been killed in the Alps until the disaster on the Matterhorn. T. S. Kennedy, in a letter the following day, was the first to point out the real lessons of the accident—that 'a large party should always be divided into threes, or, at the most, fours,' and that it was 'necessary to protest against the practice of inexperienced men ascending difficult peaks'. Outside the columns of *The Times*, comment was more unrestrained and more uninformed. There were protests against 'these senseless and purposeless Alp climbings'. It was proposed that the Alpine Club should 'at least order that in future no hired guides shall accompany Englishmen bent on distinguishing themselves in achieving dangerous ascents'. The *Pall Mall Gazette*, the *Saturday Evening Post*, and the *Evening Standard* all took up the cry, their loudness being in almost direct proportion to their ignorance.

'When a nation is bitten with a peculiar passion,' said the *Illustrated London News*, 'it seldom passes out without trouble and painful experiences, and though one or two young men are knocked up for life each year by hill climbing, it is by no means certain that a member of the Alpine Club will not endeavour to surmount a 'virgin peak' of some wonderous mountain in 1875 and render a family heirless and a mother unhappy for life.' Ruskin, preparing a new Preface for *Sesame and Lilies*, commented that 'We need not, it seems to me, loudly blame anyone for paying a guide to take a brave walk with him. Therefore, gentlemen of the Alpine Club, as much danger as you care to face, by all means; but, if you please, not so much talk of it. The real ground for reprehension of Alpine climbing is that, with less cause, it excites more vanity than any other athletic skill.' Nevertheless, Ruskin joined the Club four years later.

From those who realised that mountaineering would continue anyway, there came in August 1865 a fine crop of suggestions, ranging from the proposal that climbers should not tic together but merely hold the rope, an idea which caused one mountaineer to 'shudder at the idea of the mischief which might be caused' by it. There were proposals that wire—on an analogy drawn from picture wire—might be used in the rope, while one writer described a system of mobile handrails of almost Munchausen audacity which appears to have been initiated by a local man described in a subsequent letter as 'the most unblushing liar in the Dauphine'.

Yet it would be untrue to suggest that interest rested entirely on the loss of four lives. Even for the comparatively well-informed *Times* readers, considerable mystery remained. *The Times* itself had got off to an unfortunate start. Its first announcement had reported three men killed, one of them a 'Rev. Mr. Hudson', a statement that brought forth a letter from John Alfred Hudson, a barrister, hastily informing all readers that he was still alive. This first account of the accident had come from the *Journal de Genève*, with its order of descent as Croz, Lord Francis Douglas, Hadow, Hudson and Whymper. M'Cormick's letter, published the following day and written in ignorance of the Geneva report, merely confused the issue to all except the most careful readers, and on August 2nd, *The Times* reported that it was 'requested to state, upon the best authority, that Lord Francis Douglas did not make the fatal slip which caused the lamentable accident on the Matterhorn.' It was perhaps this which induced 'A Friend of One of the Victims' to write asking: 'Why did Mr. Hudson leave behind him the apparatus which it is said he had prepared purposely for this difficult ascent? Who made the fatal slip which caused the catastrophe? These and other questions await answers which only Mr. Whymper can give with certainty.' The same attitude was shown by Alexander Rivington, a member of the Alpine Club who started his letter to *The Times* with: 'While we await some details from Mr. Whymper ...'

During the week that followed *The Times* leader, Whymper therefore had every inducement to make some statement. He had already been approached by the Alpine Club, in the person of the Rev. Hereford George who wrote to him saying: 'Let me implore you not to delay as I think it absolutely necessary such a narrative should appear.' Many friends urged the same thing privately. But Whymper still hesitated, held back both by general reluctance and by the feeling that whatever he did would bring a fame to the Taugwalders which he felt they did not deserve.

While he considered the matter he took advice of three people. The first of these was Dr., later Bishop, George Forrest Browne, an old friend of Hudson and an ecclesiastic who was to become President of the Alpine Club. 'As Whymper had got into the way of consulting me about matters other than Alpine, I was the first person to whom he gave a full account of what really took place,' he later wrote. 'He came to see me in Cambridge. He had sealed up the bag in which he had the remains of the rope. He came to consult me on two questions of casuistry, on at least one of which he did not take my advice.' The details of this story must be viewed with an extremely sceptical eye, since the Bishop's account of how Tyndall sought Douglas's body on the rocks of the Matterhorn is greatly, and demonstrably, different from Tyndall's own version. However, the story was subsequently saved from decent burial by no less a person than Lord Conway of Allington, himself among the greatest of the second generation of mountaineers. By the time that Bishop Browne was relaying the story to Conway—about half a century after the accident—it was Zermatt, and not Cambridge, where the meeting had taken place. Conway added, moreover, a gloss of three sentences which adds to the considerable obfuscation of the Bishop Browne evidence. 'It happened,' he wrote, 'that Whymper was the last man in the party and could not actually see Hadow's slip and Croz's overthrow by him, but two or three strands of the rope might have been severed beforehand without anyone knowing. The end of the rope would have retained some sign of the cutting. The end engraved in *Scrambles* is not the one where the breakage occurred. It is the right rope, but not the broken end.'

It is difficult to see any justification for Conway's implication. Had Whymper, in fact, had physical evidence—ie a rope which 'retained some sign of the cutting'—rather than the hypothetical evidence of what might have gone on in Taugwalder's mind when he tied up—there is no reason to suppose that he would have concealed it. Rather the reverse. It is also curious that the suggestion should be made of weakening a rope which, according to all the evidence, needed no weakening anyway.

The trouble, of course, is not that old men forget but that they are apt to remember, with the best will in the world, slightly out of focus. Thus with the rope in the *Scrambles*. From the binding shown on it, it seems quite clear that the illustration of 'rope broken on the Matterhorn'— which is Whymper's description—is merely one portion of the rope, much of which was chopped up into small lengths for fixed ropes during the descent. He never claimed it to be anything more.

The work of this particular red herring was complicated by that of a companion. For Bishop Browne specifically claimed to Conway that 'he was the only living man who knew the truth about the accident, and that that knowledge would perish with him'. Now from a later statement made by Conway it appears that the first part of this claim was half correct but that the truth was concerned not with the accident itself but with its aftermath. For Browne's secret almost certainly referred to a statement made by Whymper in August to John Jermyn Cowell, who had been Honorary Secretary to the Alpine Club the previous year; and Browne was not to know that Whymper had put the statement on record and that it would subsequently come to light in his papers. It is just remotely possible that the Bishop was told by Whymper some significant fact about the accident itself. But there is no evidence of this; moreover, if it were the case, then Whymper must have concealed it for years; so must old Peter and so must his son—all of them presumably keeping quiet, if not actually lying, with a dexterity and success which would call for wonder. Commonsense suggests that Browne was as confused on this point as he was about Tyndall. He was, after all, into his eighties when he wrote his *Recollections* and apparently well into his nineties when he reminisced with Conway. As Farrar said, we are all human.

Yet if we must discount the accuracy of the details it would be unwise to disregard Browne's plain 'he came to see me'. It seems very likely that Whymper did in fact go to see him. And it is probable that one of the 'two questions of casuistry' which Browne mentions concerned the attitude which Whymper should take to the actions, or assumed actions, of the Taugwalders—which Whymper believed went far beyond old Peter's choice of rope. Browne's advice would probably have been to accuse the Taugwalders openly or to keep quiet. Whymper did neither.

Instead, he visited Cowell, and his brother John W. Cowell. Just what he said to them is not entirely clear. But a memorandum by the Cowells found among Whymper's papers has Whymper spending the night following the accident with the Taugwalders facing him 'with his back to a rock and with his axe in his hand to order them to keep at a greater distance from him'. The nub of the memorandum lies in one sentence: 'The inferences which arose in our minds from what E. Whymper described were that the Taugwalders saw that the additional loss of Whymper would afford them an opening to a future notoriety of a very lucrative nature, and that they were prepared to avail themselves of any opportunity which might offer during the descent of bringing about that loss—and Edward Whymper did not deny to us that similar inferences suggested themselves to him during the whole of that dreadful night.'

Whatever Whymper's exact words to the Cowells, they formed, in practice, no purely private communication. The same day Cowell was repeating the substance of the story to Oscar Browning, another member of the Club, who noted that 'the next morning Whymper's narrative appeared in *The Times*, omitting some things which he had told to Cowell'. It is possible, although unlikely, that the Cowells misinterpreted Whymper's words, or his attitude; it is easy to imagine how a difference of language and the aftermath of disaster distorted events in the mind of a young man of 25. But it is certain that as the unsubstantiated, if inferred, libel on the guides seeped out over the years it did Whymper little good.

The date of the meeting between Whymper and the Cowells is not known. But on August 7th he received a letter from Mr. Wills, the President of the Alpine Club. 'Give your own account,' he was advised, 'let it be truthful, manly and unflinching—wherever blame is due (if blame there be) let it rest—but do not let people go on conjecturing the worst, when you could silence the greater part of it by your utterance. To some extent also the Club is on its trial. People are daily writing to abuse us and our doings.'

This letter at last roused Whymper from his self imposed silence, and there is a strong presumption that he came up to London on the 7th and met both Wills and the Cowells. He was certainly at last induced to put his account of the accident on paper. It was dated from Haslemere, August 7th and was published in *The Times* the following day with an accompanying letter from Wills, also dated the 7th, which helped to explain the delay.

Whymper's letter occupied two full columns and it told the story which he was to tell for the rest of his life. It explained that no rope was taken from Zermatt in view of what had been cached at the Schwarzsee. As to the reasons for leaving Hudson's wire rope—'I do not know; it was not mentioned by Mr. Hudson, and at that time I had not even seen it.' He then came to the accident.

'As far as I know, at the moment of the accident no one was actually moving. I cannot speak with certainty, neither can the Taugwalders, because the two leading men were partially hidden from our sight by an intervening mass of rock. Poor Croz had laid aside his axe, and in order to give Mr. Hadow greater security was absolutely taking hold of his legs and putting his feet, one by one, into their proper positions. From the movements of their shoulders it is my belief that Croz, having done as I have said, was in the act of turning round to go down a step or two himself; at this moment Mr. Hadow slipped, fell on him, and knocked him over. I heard one startled exclamation from Croz, then saw him and Mr. Hadow flying downwards; in another moment Hudson was dragged from his steps and Lord F. Douglas immediately after him. All this was the work of a moment; but immediately we heard Croz's exclamation, Taugwalder and myself planted ourselves as firmly as the rocks would permit; the rope was tight between us, and the shock came on us both as on one man. We held; but the rope broke midway between Taugwalder and Lord F. Douglas.'

He had been forced to mention the Taugwalders. But he made certain that they would reap no rewards from his letter to the papers. 'The two men, paralysed by terror, cried like infants,' he said, 'and trembled in such a manner as to threaten us with the fate of the others. Immediately we had descended to a safe place, I asked for the rope that had broken, and to my surprise—indeed, to my horror—found that it was the weakest of the three ropes.' He added that when the bodies were discovered he found to his astonishment that there was only one weak link—that between Taugwalder and Lord Francis Douglas. And he added that he had not received answers to the questions he had requested should be put to old Peter. This accusation against a man who would, in the circumstances, have little chance of effective reply, raised small comment at the time.

The following day *The Times* published a second leading article, congratulating Whymper on his 'interesting and affecting narrative', and commenting, with some charity in view of his statements, that 'the guides were first-rate'. Whymper's letter had, as Wills said the same day, stripped 'the calamity of all mystery and doubt'.

All that remained now was for Whymper—and the Taugwalders—to live through the aftermath.

CHAPTER TWELVE

THE ABIDING QUESTIONS

W HYMPERS' LETTER TO *The Times*, together with the leading article of the following day and Wills's letter underlining that the affair had now been stripped 'of all mystery and doubt', wrote a public finis to the discussion which had simmered away for three weeks. All appeared to have been simply solved by the fact that a guide had—with or without intent—chosen a weak rope. Of the innocent public, few now stopped to consider that had there been no such weak rope seven instead of four men would almost certainly have fallen to their deaths; few asked why an inexperienced youth such as Hadow had been taken on the expedition, or asked who was really in charge. It must have seemed, by the middle of August 1865, that the tale was told.

Yet the Matterhorn accident refused to fade away. It continued to exercise men's minds, to excite them, to make them ask questions. There were a number of reasons for this, not least of which was that on the Matterhorn men had been staking out yet another claim on the unstaked property of nature, a process for which the Victorians had a somewhat uncritical enthusiasm. Secondly, as the story was considered over the years a shimmer of doubt began to gather once more over some details of the disaster, and these were later probed with the indefatigable energy of Alpine scholarship. In the general and uninformed mind this doubt appeared, quite wrongly, to hint at some hidden skullduggery; it was perhaps felt that if the members of the Swiss Enquiry saw fit to remain quiet there must, after all, be something to conceal. Added to this there grew throughout the years the feeling that while Whymper had not himself hidden anything of relevance to the accident or its causes, there was nevertheless a simple selecting of facts in his story which gave interest to any new details. There were to be many of these. Finally, Edward Whymper himself helped in no uncertain way to keep the Matterhorn story alive; writing about it, lecturing about it, and doing little to dissuade the public from feeling that here, in the person of the stern, leonine headed Whymper, they were seeing something of the inner iron which had been transferred from the mountains to the man himself.

Three abiding questions thus remain to be answered. What was the effect of the Matterhorn accident on the development of mountaineering? What was its effect on Whymper, on the two Taugwalders? And— the ultimate question—was the whole truth ever told?

After the accident, mountaineering could never be quite the same, although for reasons more complex than are sometimes thought. The Matterhorn was not, as we have seen, the last great unclimbed peak of the Alps. The highest point on the Grandes Jorasses was reached only in 1868, the lower summit of the Meije climbed in 1870 and the highest not until 1877. It was only from this period onwards that the Chamonix Aiguilles were conquered, one after another, by a new generation of mountaineers for whom the Matterhorn disaster was a tale told by their fathers. Yet in spite of all these things there is much truth in the popular generalisation that the ascent of the Matterhorn marked the end of the 'Golden Age' of mountaineering, since new factors came increasingly into play after 1865. From this date onwards there was, to a growing extent, the ascent of old mountains by new—and usually harder—routes. Men looked for the conquest of a peak not by the simplest route but by one particular face or ridge. They raised to the status of genuinely separate mountains peaks which had previously been considered as but parts of larger ones. Mountaineering by women, already practised in 1865 by such rare pioneers as Lucy Walker, was given impetus by enthusiasts of the calibre of Miss Brevoort, aunt of the Rev. W. A. B. Coolidge and, somewhat later, by Mrs. Aubrey Le Blonde, to mention only two of the many. Coolidge himself began to plough the almost untouched field of Alpine history, while there sprang up from the 1860s onwards, both in Europe and in other Continents, clubs, associations and similar organisations whose members were devoted to the exploration of mountain ranges other than the Alps—the Pyrenees, the mountains of Norway, the White Mountains and the Appalachians. None of these developments was connected with the conquest of the Matterhorn, but they combined to make the picture of the mountaineering world after 1865 very different from what it had been during the previous two decades.

All this tended to give to the Matterhorn affair an importance in the development of mountaineering that was not genuinely its due. Coolidge, writing more than 40 years later and thinking back to 1865 when he had been a boy of 15, wrote that after the accident English climbers 'went about under a sort of dark shade, looked on with scarcely disguised contempt by the world of ordinary travellers'. Captain Farrar, in a much-quoted phrase, wrote more than half a century after the accident that the deaths of Hudson and Croz had 'held up the tide of mountaineering for fully half a generation of man'.

It is doubtful if this is quite true. The first ascent of the Matterhorn stands on a historical watershed; it did not create one—so far, at least, as mountaineering and mountaineers themselves are concerned. Yet outside this purely domestic field, the events of July 1865 had one important result. They pushed the still developing sport into the light of public criticism, and enabled its merits as well as its defects to be publicly debated. In this respect the outcry was comparable to the great debate on evolution which had been brought into the open by Darwin a few years previously. Darwin had pulled together a thousand loose strands and woven them into a theory. The loose strands had been there before, visible to at least a few people, but it was only their fusing and development into *The Origin of Species* which brought them into the light of public debate. In a comparable way men had been risking their lives on mountains, without benefit of scientific excuse, for at least two decades before

1865; yet the Matterhorn accident drew the subject of mountaineering into the open and provided a reason not only for those anxious to attack it but for those who wished to explain why men climbed mountains, enduring hardship and danger, for what appeared to be the slimmest of reasons, or for no reason at all.

In 1870 Lucy Walker made the first ascent of the Matterhorn by a woman; a few weeks later she was followed by Miss Brevoort who, having lost this tempting 'first', won the consolation prize of the first woman's traverse, ascending from Zermatt and descending to Breuil. Her nephew, the Rev. W. A. B. Coolidge, secured as a trophy a portion of Croz's blouse which still fluttered as a reminder of the first ascent. The Matterhorn was still, as it always will be, a peak where death can strike suddenly and surely; yet it was already being carried along that path of progress which in a famous phrase leads a mountain from being 'the most difficult peak in the Alps' to 'an easy day for a lady'. 'When Whymper climbed it again in 1874, his ascent was the 76th; by the end of the next summer but one, during which he climbed to the tent platform on which Hudson and his own party had slept, the 141st had been made. So far as mountaineering in general was concerned, *the day the rope broke* had marked merely the end of one stage in the evolving pattern of mountaineering and the beginning of another. In the story of the mountain it was the day that had opened the door.

Yet the history of the inanimate is trifling compared with the lives of breathing creatures, especially, from our viewpoint, the lives of human beings. The effects of the Matterhorn accident on the three survivors are therefore of intriguing interest, especially as these effects were so diverse.

Young Peter survived an initial unreasoning suspicion among some of the guides which implicated him in the accident even though, as last man on the rope, he could not have been directly involved. Whymper's letter in *The Times* claiming that he and his father had, 'paralysed by terror, cried like infants' after the accident, seems to have made singularly little impression on possible employers. They continued to engage him, and young Peter quickly became the acknowledged expert of the Swiss face of the Matterhorn, climbing the mountain more than a hundred times.

With old Peter the story was very different. He did not completely live down the libellous implications of Whymper's story, for which Whymper was never able to bring any evidence whatsoever, and which he must have known it would be impracticable for Taugwalder to refute. It is not necessary to condemn Whymper for this; the facts suffice. Old Peter left Switzerland in the years following the accident and settled in the United States. He eventually returned to Zermatt and died, shortly afterwards, in 1888, at the hotel at the Schwarzsee which had by this time been opened by the Seiler family.

On Edward Whymper the effects are more debatable. There is little doubt that he was much moved by the death of Croz—'tears do not often come out of my eyes', he wrote almost half a century later, 'but when I think of the miserable end of this grand guide, they come out.' But the change in his mountaineering efforts had apparently been de-cided upon before the accident. 'He had resolved to do the Matterhorn, and equally resolved, when that was done, to give up mountaineering, because there were no more new great mountains to be conquered', the Rev. F. J. A. Hort wrote to his wife on August 1st, 1865, after a long talk with Girdlestone. Nevertheless, the effects of the tragedy were deep and lasting, even though rarely revealed. 'I have always regarded this acci-dent as arising from divided responsibility, through no *one* person being in command of the party', Whymper wrote in 1894. 'Ever afterwards I have travelled alone.' And to a young enquirer three years later he com-mented, 'you've got strong legs, but remember that in the Alps one does not march only with one's legs but also with one's head'.

Whymper returned to the Alps in the summer of 1866, but he re-turned only to set three men digging a trench in the névé on the Col de Valpelline to give fresh information on the structure of glaciers. 'I did not go out wishing to make ascents or passes, having as you may suppose not quite so much appetite for this sort of thing as I had, but I went out nevertheless for definite objects, and I got as hard scrambling and walking as ever I have had', he wrote to the Rev. James Robertson in September 1866. 'I have done with the Alps now and am getting rid of my properties, which looks as if I meant it.'

If he was 'done with the Alps', he was not done with exploration, and in 1867 he realised his ambition of visiting Greenland. His journey was planned with great skill but dogged by bad luck. He accomplished less than he hoped, although his report was subsequently published by the British Association, and he returned to Greenland five years later. Yet for thousands of people Edward Whymper remained until his death the man of the Matterhorn. Few had even heard of Charles Hudson and there is much truth in old Seiler's comment in later years when it was remarked that the Matterhorn was Whymper's great 'bêtise'. "It was the making of him", he replied. Such was indeed to be the case. For whoever might climb the Matterhorn, whatever new and brilliant assaults might be made on its ridges or faces, there was always in the background the craggy unbending figure of Edward Whymper. He, after all, was one of the men who had broken through the barrier. He was unwilling to let people forget the fact.

Whymper began writing the *Scrambles* on his return from Greenland in 1867. He intended it to describe his adventures in the Alps and to culminate with the ascent of the Matterhorn. He worked on it for three years, writing and re-writing, cutting, adding, deleting, polishing, until the rough mass of his experiences had been hewn into a literary masterpiece.

The book was to be illustrated, and in 1869 he began asking acquaintances in the Alpine Club for photographs; these were to be utilised for a drawing entitled 'The Clubroom of Zermatt', which would show Club members outside the Monte Rosa. There were difficulties, as he explained to Robertson to whom he wrote for a portrait in 1869. 'In my younger days I got dreadfully snubbed once or twice for intruding myself without introductions and now in consequence I am perhaps unreasonably particular', he said before describing the book. This was, he went on, 'entirely personal, all ego. The title is religiously guarded at present on account of the extreme difficulty of finding a new one should any un-principled person snap it up. It will have a hundred illustrations—the best your humble servant knows how to produce, and they will contain enough sensations for half a dozen volumes.'

Scrambles Amongst the Alps In the Years 1860–1869 was published by John Murray in the summer of 1871. Its second edition appeared two years later. There were three more before the end of the century, while a shilling edition in which photographs replaced the original Whymper illustrations appeared in 1908; another, with maps, photographs and some of Whymper's originals, appeared in 1936. It was translated into French and German, pirated in other languages, and quickly became the classic account of an heroic age.

The book is a work of art from which there still comes the thunder of the falling rocks. It has its lapses, but from it as a whole there rises up a three dimensional picture of the great age of Alpine climbing which was already over when it was published. The book deals with the whole of Whymper's early mountaineering career, but it is primarily the story of the Matterhorn to which it leads with unerring skill, and it is the story of the Matterhorn that it has kept alive ever since. The reasons for this lie not only in the drama of the story which Whymper had to tell, but in the opportunity which his tailoring of the record left for the discovery of new and significant facts, for speculation, and for explanation. He told the story as that of Edward Whymper's conquest of the Matterhorn, and in the telling he ruthlessly cut away extraneous detail. Thus no indica-tion is given that Douglas had, in fact, planned to climb the mountain, and the impression remains that he was, by Whymper's kindness, in-vited to join the attempt. The vital question of the ropes is, as two ex-perts have put it,' bedevilled by a certain vagueness on Whymper's part'. He makes the barest reference to the Enquiry—'after my examination before the court of enquiry'—and ignores the critical aftermath. None of this deserves censure. When he wrote the *Scrambles* Whymper was selecting facts with the eye of the painter rather than producing a photo-

'The Clubroom of Zermatt', Whymper's illustration from Scrambles. Old Peter
Taugwalder is seated second from right

graphic image. The result was a work of literature rather than a historical
record. Yet this very fact helped to keep the Matterhorn accident before
the eyes of the specialists as, decade by decade, new information from
diaries, letters, and personal reminiscence floated into view.

In the *Scrambles* Whymper also laid up a rod in pickle for his own
memory. Into the mouth of young Peter Taugwalder he put the quoted
words 'We don't wish you to pay us. We wish you to write in the hotel-
book at Zermatt, and to your journals, that we have not been paid,' an
interpretation which now appears to be somewhat different from the
one he had described to his colleagues in Zermatt six years previously, a
fact that was no doubt known and remembered by them. And after describing how the sash line had been used only between Lord Francis
Douglas and old Peter, he commented that 'this had a very ugly look for
Taugwalder'. His footnote stating that he had not received from M.
Clemenz the answers to questions intended to let Taugwalder clear himself may have been well meant; it further blackened the old man's name.

In 1871 Alpine *pietas* tended to stifle criticism of Whymper. Thus Leslie Stephen, then editor of the *Alpine Journal*, reviewed *The Scrambles* there with considerable praise. Yet in *Macmillan's Magazine* Stephen wrote a far more searching commentary in which he came determinedly to the defence of the Taugwalders. He pointed out that Whymper had denounced the idea that old Peter had cut the rope. 'But I rather regret,' he continued, that 'he should not reject decidedly another grave, though less serious accusation, which comes in fact to this, that Taugwalder intentionally used a weak rope in fastening himself to Lord F. Douglas. Knowing the carelessness too often displayed on such occasions, the confidence which guides will show in weak ropes, and the probable state of excitement of the whole party, which would easily account for such oversight, I think that the hypothesis of deliberate intention on Taugwalder's part is in the highest degree improbable; and there is not a particle of direct evidence in its favour.' There was none when Stephen wrote those words nearly a century ago and there is none today.

It is clear that Croz, at least, should have shared any odium which sprang from the order of roping-up. And any impartial enquirer would have pointed out that Whymper himself had tied on to Taugwalder shortly after the descent had begun, that Whymper had provided the ropes, and that Whymper should at least have borne his share of the responsibility for failing to note that the next link down from the man on to whom he was physically being tied was provided by the weakest of his own three ropes.

Whymper omitted from the *Scrambles* any reference to his statements to the Cowells, no doubt hating second thoughts about what Lunn has called 'the criminal irresponsibility with which [he] committed to paper a charge of attempted murder, which was unsupported by a shred of evidence'. He paid tribute to Taugwalder—'not only was his act at the critical moment wonderful as a feat of strength, but it was admirable in its performance at the right time'. Yet he did deal with the choice of ropes so that years later men still spoke of the 'duty to vindicate Taugwalder's good name'. Youth and inexperience were no doubt among the reasons for Whymper's conduct; yet some further explanation is necessary and it must lie either in some act of the Taugwalders which Whymper concealed or in the character of the writer himself.

The *Scrambles* brought Whymper the Order of SS Maurice and Lazarus from the King of Italy. It confirmed his position in Britain as the most adventurous mountaineer of the great age that had ended. He lectured. And he formally warned off his old colleague C. E. Mathews from using the title *'Scrambles in the Alps'* for the talks which Mathews was giving to small local societies—'I have been his friend for more than 25 years', Mathews wrote in amazement to Conway. He described his mountaineering experiences in magazines and newspapers, and was a constant illustrator of the mountaineering and quasi-mountaineering volumes which now began to roll from the presses in increasing numbers.

It would, however, be wrong to write off Whymper's achievements after the age of 25, for he combined to a rare degree the qualities of showman and serious enquirer. By the 1870s men were climbing farther afield, to ever greater heights, and it was to Whymper that there fell the work of adding to the information on how men might live and move at great altitudes. In 1879 he left England for the Andes of Ecuador. With him went no English companions—he was allergic to most of them, and the feeling was frequently reciprocated; instead he had Jean-Antoine Carrel, the most competent and reliable man on a mountain whom he knew, and Jean-Antoine's cousin Louis Carrel. Like most of the other tasks that Whymper tackled, this one was tackled successfully. He made the first and second ascents of Chimborazo, travelled extensively, and spent 36 nights above 14,000 feet. The products of his journey, reported in *Travels amongst the Great Andes of the Equator* and in a volume of scientific appendices, were workmanlike and useful. So was the investigation which he later carried out on compressed food for explorers. So was his work on the aneroid barometer—and so were the guidebooks to Zermatt and Chamonix which he later wrote and which continued to be printed, edition after edition, throughout the later years of his life.

All this was worth while, all of it was well done. For anyone other than Edward Whymper, the man whose star had blazed up after the dramatic events of 1865, it would have been success. And yet. 'There is little to choose between the styles of his writing in 1865 and 1890 when he had doubled his age', said his biographer, Frank Smythe, in a book which is as kind to its subject as the evidence can be made to allow. 'It was the same with his art. Neither in style nor in imaginative conception did he advance on his work as a young man. He gained in experience and knowledge, yet his creative abilities remained on a single plane.'

There seems little doubt that this was due to the traumatic effect of the Matterhorn accident. It had brought him fame; it had provided him with an ever ready market for his articles and his lectures. Yet it had also halted him in his tracks so that even in the 20th century he continued to be the determined mountaineer whose efforts had ended an heroic age in an hour of mingled triumph and disaster. Thus he remained, whatever his achievements, like a fly fixed in amber, a record of things past. Courage and honesty both continued to shine from his character, yet he remained an unclubbable man. Lunn's comment that '. . . Whymper did not like Taugwalder, and it is highly probable that Taugwalder did not like Whymper. Few people did,' may include a touch of the acid, but it is difficult to believe that it was not true. Whymper himself, writing to Coolidge in the 1880s, admitted that 'I fear there must be something queer about me or some fault which sorely needs correction and which I will correct if you as a true and kind friend will point it out'. After the Matterhorn accident he preferred to climb only with professional guides, a reasonable enough preference in the circumstances, yet one which appears to have been inherent, and merely strengthened by the disaster. He travelled alone. He had few confidants—though he was in the habit of sending Christmas cards to young mountaineers inscribed 'from the old lion to the new'. And his marriage in 1906 at the age of 66 to a woman 45 years his junior, was the failure that many must have prophesied.

Yet in his qualities as well as in his defects, Whymper ran true to the end. During his sixties, he made three exploratory journeys to the Rockies for the Canadian Pacific Railway. His attitude to guides had remained

The memorial to Whymper on the wall of the Hotel Monte Rosa, Zermatt

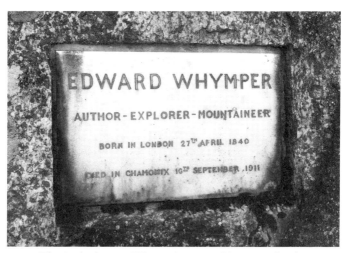

The simple plaque on Whymper's grave at Chamonix where he died on Spetember 16th 1911

unchanged by the onward stumble of democratic ideas and there was much trouble, yet his indomitable will continued to achieve results even— on the last expedition—at the age of 69. Two years later he planned to visit Coolidge with whom he had become reconciled after a bitter, libel-threatening, dispute about the accuracy of an illustration in the *Scrambles*. 'When I come, I shall come in the old style', he wrote in quavering hand. 'Shall walk up, not order rooms in advance, and take my chance as to finding a room. If none can be had, I shall camp out.' He arrived at Coolidge's Chalet Montana on September 3rd, 1911, spent most of the day refighting old battles, and left in the evening for Zermatt. He went on to Geneva, then to Chamonix where a few days later he fell ill, locked himself in his room, refused all aid, and died on September 16th.

It now seemed unlikely that anything more would ever be known about the events of that distant July afternoon in 1865. Yet the echoes continued to be heard.

A year before his death, Whymper had written to Alexander Jullien of Geneva, with whom he was preparing a new edition of the *Scrambles* and of his *Guide to Zermatt*. Would he, Whymper asked, try to get from the Valais authorities a copy of the evidence given before the Court of Enquiry held in Zermatt 45 years previously, together with the findings? Jullien was unsuccessful, but a few years later the attempt was renewed by Henry Montagnier, an American student of Alpine history. This time, following the advice of M. Jean-Ch. de Courten, the cantonal judge at Sion, the authorities agreed. The records of the official Enquiry were at last released. The year was 1920.

They told the story we know today. And they revealed that the members of the Enquiry had decided, in effect, that there was nothing for them to decide. On the facts which they had elicited from the witnesses they had felt it possible to be certain of two things. No one had done anything blameworthy; and Mr. Hadow had been the cause of the accident. As a result there was no reason to follow up the Enquiry; no more need be done. Thus was old Peter acquitted by implication, 55 years later, of the act with which he had never been publicly charged.

Young Peter, by this time in his seventies, had already given his somewhat belated story, although this had not yet seen the light of day. For the same Montagnier who had at last winkled the report of the Enquiry from the Valais authorities had in 1917 sent a man to obtain a statement from young Peter in Zermatt. The original document appears to have been lost, but from a translation it seems likely that it was written not by young Peter himself but by the interviewer, who possibly added his own literary trimmings, and was then signed by the guide. It was published only in 1957, with annotations by D. F. O. Dangar and T. S. Blakeney, in a work of scholarship which is a masterpiece of its kind. Memory worked a few inconsistencies into young Peter's story, as it did into Whymper's when he aged, but the general lines followed those already known.

It was now becoming ever clearer that the drama of the Matterhorn and its first ascent had lain in the clean clear struggle of man and mountain and the almost Grecian manner in which whatever Gods may be had taken their revenge. It was not to remain thus, unembroidered. As events slipped into distant history after Whymper's death, the story was to be used as a vehicle for more than one ingenious human plot. In 1929 Carl Haensel in his *Der Kampf ums Matterhorn* joined Whymper in a semi mystical friendship with Lord Francis Douglas—so that Claire-Eliane Engel, a noted student of mountain literature, wondered 'whether the author was not influenced by the fact that Francis Douglas was Lord Alfred Douglas's uncle'. A great radio play of the accident, *Flags on the Matterhorn*, heightened the sense of drama. *The Challenge* was a film which used the bare bones of the story as the basis for telling a good tale, while a German author described the accident on the assumption that Croz and young Peter were rivals in love. Little wonder that the rumours continued, that their survival was implied as late as 1957 when the annotators of young Peter's narrative noted that 'probably few people today believe these stories'.

Has the complete truth been told, even now? The answer, with one rider that is of only academic importance when placed beside the wild stories of cut or deliberately chosen ropes, is almost certainly yes.

There are minor discrepancies in the accounts told over the decades by Whymper, by old Peter and by his son. But two things should be remembered. These discrepancies are of the sort that do arise when memory casts back to great events, and their very existence helps to discount any suggestions that all three men might have been telling a concocted tale. Such discounting is in fact hardly necessary. In certain circumstances it would be conceivable that three men had maintained a prearranged story through thick and thin; in this case the language difficulty, and the mutual dislike of Whymper and the Taugwalders which developed, would alone have been enough to prevent this—quite apart from the strong moral fibre of Whymper himself and the character of the Taugwalders, against which no valid case has ever been made.

One must therefore assume that the order of descent, the sudden slip, the actual breaking of the rope, all took place as they have been recorded. And there has, it should be stressed, never been any evidence whatsoever that the culpable rope was weakened; indeed, the whole gravamen of Whymper's implied charge was that, even without interference, it was too weak for the task for which it was used. As for the choice of rope, Leslie Stephen's comment that there was 'not a particle of direct evidence to favour the theory of deliberate choice by Taugwalder' rings as true today as it did in 1871. Barring the unearthing of new evidence, which seems in the highest degree unlikely, it must therefore be concluded that the whole tale has now been told.

Only on one point does doubt remain. It must be remembered that none of the three survivors saw clearly the details of the initial slip on the mountain; that old Peter, re-examined at the Enquiry with the observation that he had been contradicting Whymper, withdrew his original story that the rope had broken between himself and Lord Francis Douglas before, rather than after, Croz had been pulled or pushed from his steps. No one is certain. In the circumstances, no one could be. But it seems just possible that the course of events during the seconds which followed the initial slip were different from those which are now generally accepted. It seems just possible that Hadow's slip pulled Hudson from his steps but failed to dislodge Croz; that Hudson in turn pulled down Lord Francis Douglas; that the rope broke between Douglas and Taugwalder; and that for an instant Croz sustained them all, a Titan holding three lives in his hands until, with the word 'impossible' on his lips, he too was dragged from his steps to destruction. It is a picture which would provide a fitting end to a great guide.

Thus the 'guilt' of the Matterhorn story, if guilt it can be called, is less sensational, more human, than would be provided by any criminal act. It arises from hot blood driving out cool reason, from the impingement of circumstance on able young men, anxious to succeed, contemptuous of caution, over confident against the Fates. The tragedy of Hudson and Douglas, of Hadow and Croz—and of the survivors—was a tragedy not of evil intent but of human aspiration itself. It is thus both more tragic and yet more bearable.

BIBLIOGRAPHY

MANUSCRIPT SOURCES

Foreign Office files, Public Record Office, London.

Coolidge archives, Zentralbibliothek, Zürich.

Diaries of Professor John Tyndall and of Thomas Hirst, Royal Institution, London.

Letters of the Rev. A. G. Girdlestone, Alpine Club, London.

Letters of Edward Whymper, Alpine Club, London.

PRINTED SOURCES

Among journals, the *Alpine Journal* from 1863 onwards provides by far the most important single source of information relating to the Matterhorn accident. It contains, in addition to many scores of minor references and details, a number of important papers on special aspects of the accident, the most valuable of which are mentioned below.

Most other Alpine journals have during the last 90 years or more contained information bearing on the accident, some of it reliable, some of it not.

The *Echo des Alpes* (Geneva, 1867), *Journal de Genève* (Geneva, 1865), *The Times* (London, 1865) all contain material bearing on the accident, as do many other journals, and newspapers of July and August, 1865. Additional details were given by Whymper himself in magazine and newspaper articles during the following years, among the last of these being one published in the *Strand Magazine* (Rine of January, 1909.

Brown, T. Graham, *Girdlestone and the Matterhorn Accident*, 1865, *Alpine Journal*, LXVII, May, 1950.

Browne, the Right Rev. G. F., *The Recollections of a Bishop*, 1915.

Browning, Oscar, *Memories of Sixty Years*, 1910.

Conway of Allington, Lord, *Episodes in a Varied Life*, 1932.

Coolidge, the Rev. W. A. B., *Swiss Travel and Swiss Guidebooks*, 1889.

————*The Alps in Nature and History*, 1908.

————*Alpine Studies*, 1912.

Dangar, D. F. O. and Blakeney, T. S., *The First Ascent of the Matterhorn, the Narrative of 'Young' Peter Taugwalder, Alpine Journal*, May, 1957.

Egger, Carl, *Pionere der Alpen*, Zurich, 1946.

Engel, Claire-Eliane, *A History of Mountaineering in the Alps*, 1950.

Eve, Professor A. S. and Creasey, C. H., *Life and Work of John Tyndall* 1945

Farrar, Captain J. P., *Days of Long Ago, Alpine Journal*, Vol XXXII, February, 1918.

————*Report of the Accident on Mont Cervin*, 1865, *Alpine Journal*, Vol. XXXIII, November, 1920.

Girdlestone, the Rev. A. G., *The High Alps Without Guides*, 1870.

Gos, Charles, *Alpinisme Anecdotique*, Paris and Neuchatel, 1934

————*Le Cervin*, Paris and Neuchatel, 1948.

Gussfeldt, Dr. Paul, *In den Hochalpen. Erlebnisse aus den Jahren 1859-85*, Berlin, 1886.

Hort, A. F., *Life and Letters of Fenton John Anthony Hort*, 1896.

Hudson, the Rev. C. and Kennedy, E. S., *An ascent of Mont Blanc by a new route and without guides*, 1856.

Jones, the Rev. Harry, *The Regular Swiss Round*, 1865.

Klucker, Christian, *Adventures of an Alpine Guid*e, 1932.

Lunn, Arnold, *Mountain Jubilee*, 1943.

————*Zermatt and the Valais*, 1955.

————*A Century of Mountaineering*, 1957.

M'Cormick, the Rev. Joseph, *A Sad Holiday*, 1865.

Mumm, A. L. *The Alpine Club Register*, 1923-1928.

Rey, Guido, *The Matterhorn*, 1946.

Smythe, F. S., *Edward Whymper*, 1940.

Studer, Gottlieb, *Ueber Eis and Schnee; Die hochsten Gipfel der Schwez und die Geschichte ihrer Besteigung,* Berne, 1869-1870,1883.

Whymper, Edward, *Scrambles Amongst the Alps in the Years 1860-1869*, 1871.

———*Travels Amongst the Great Andes of the Equator*, 1892.

Yeats Browne, F. A., *Family Notes*, Florence, 1917.